HALEY'S CLEANING HINTS

GRAHAM *and* ROSEMARY HALEY

Illustrations
by
DAVID McNIVEN

New American Library

New American Library
Published by New American Library, a division of
Penguin Group (USA) Inc., 375 Hudson Street,
New York, New York 10014, U.S.A.
Penguin Books Ltd, 80 Strand,
London WC2R 0RL, England
Penguin Books Australia Ltd, 250 Camberwell Road,
Camberwell, Victoria 3124, Australia
Penguin Books Canada Ltd, 10 Alcorn Avenue,
Toronto, Ontario, Canada M4V 3B2
Penguin Books (N.Z.) Ltd, Cnr Rosedale and Airborne Roads,
Albany, Auckland 1310, New Zealand

Penguin Books Ltd, Registered Offices:
80 Strand, London WC2R 0RL, England

Published by New American Library, a division of Penguin Group (USA) Inc. Previously
published in a 3H Productions edition.

First New American Library Printing, April 2004
10 9 8 7 6 5 4 3 2 1

Copyright © 3H Productions Inc., 2000
All rights reserved

Printed in the United States of America

PUBLISHER'S NOTE
Accordingly nothing in this book is intended as an express or implied warranty of the
suitability or fitness of any product, service or design. The reader wishing to use a product,
service or design discussed in this book should first consult a specialist or professional to
ensure suitability and fitness for the reader's particular lifestyle and environmental needs.

It's really the satisfaction, you know . . .

Your boss's wife just spilled her glass of Cabernet on your $200 tablecloth. You don't think of the money. You just enjoy the look on her face...as you remove the stain in five seconds with a little ordinary borax and warm water!

You'll probably save a hundred times what you paid for this book.

A 99¢ bottle of vinegar could replace the $20 you'd spend on a copper and brass cleaner, a chrome cleaner, a glass cleaner and a toilet cleaner. The savings don't take too long to add up.

What fascinates us though, is the magic of it all. The look on your friends' faces as your entire silverware collection turns gleaming in ten seconds, with water softener, foil and salt! You're a hero...a household hero. But you're not the only one...

These 250 pages introduce you to the Household Heroes in your home. Ordinary items, with more than a thousand cleaning and space-saving properties, ready to rescue you in your time of need!

Haley's Cleaning Hints is our second book. Our first, *Haley's Hints,* covered topics as diverse as cooking, plumbing, pest control, even car care. However, we noticed, 400,000 copies later, that our cleaning hints were the ones most in demand.

So we know *Haley's Cleaning Hints* will become an invaluable reference source for you. But you'll also have the satisfaction of having more friends now than ever. Once they know you own this book, they'll be calling you for advice constantly!

Be kind. Share the wisdom. It's really satisfying!

Graham and Rosemary

A Small Sample Of What Your
HOUSEHOLD HEROES
Can Do For You!

Meet...

BAKING SODA

Cleans: Appliances; Bathtubs; Carpets; China; Counters; Drains; Floors; Grout; Laundry; Marble; Pots and Pans; Stains

Deodorizes: Appliances; Basements; Bathrooms; Books; Carpets; Kitchens; Laundry; Sneakers…and much more…

HAIR SPRAY

Removes: Coffee and Tea Stains; Ink Stains; Lipstick Stains; Marker on Walls; Scuff Marks on Floors and Items; Static Cling

Preserves: Kid's Artwork; Panty Hose; Copper and Brass; Cut Flowers…and much more…

VINEGAR

Cleans: Appliances; Bathtubs; Chrome; Carpets; Clothes; Crystal; Drains; Faucets; Furniture; Garbage Disposers; Humidifiers; Kettles; Laundry; Paintbrushes; Showers; Stains; Toilet Bowls…and much more…

SALT

Cleans: Carpets; Cast-Iron Pans; Chimney Creosote; Drains; Egg Spills; Grease Stains; Laundry; Perspiration Stains; Soot; Stainless-Steel Sinks; Upholstery Spills; Wicker Furniture; Wine Stains…and much more…

BORAX

Cleans: Bathtubs; Carpets; Drains; Floors; Laundry; Mildew; Pet Accidents; Stains like…Curry, Fruit, Vomit, Red Wine, Tiles, Toilet Rings, Walls…and much more…

ALUMINUM FOIL

Good For: BBQ Cleaning; Chrome Cleaning; Dryer Static; Flashlight Repair; Mixer Messes; Mirror Repair; Preserving Ice Cream; Silverware Cleaning…and much more…

SHAVING CREAM

Removes: Stains like…Blood; Chocolate; Coffee; Ketchup; Kid's Paints; Pet Accidents; Soot; Spaghetti Sauce; Tea…from Carpets; Plush Toys; Rugs

Defogs: Eyeglasses; Bathroom Mirrors; Windows…and much more…

AMMONIA

Cleans: BBQs; Chrome; Clothing; Diamonds; Faucets; Gold; Golf Balls; Ovens; Painted Walls; Shoes; Silver Jewelry; Stains like…Chocolate, Curry, Grass, Mildew, Vases…and much more…

WATER SOFTENER

Cleans: Bath Mats; Coffee Cups; Coffee-makers; Enamel Broiling Pans; Laundry; Pots with Burned Food; Painted Walls; Silverware; Thermos; Tile Mold…and much more…

WATERLESS HAND CLEANER

Removes: Stains like…Bacon Splatters; BBQ Sauce; Blood; Chocolate; Cigarette Ash; Coffee; Dirt; Egg; Eyeliner; Glue; Grass; Gravy; Grease; Iodine; Ketchup; Mascara; Mustard; Oil; Rust; Salad Dressing; Salsa; Soy Sauce; Spaghetti Sauce; Tabasco Sauce; Tea; Worcestershire Sauce…and much more…

TOOTHPASTE

Cleans: Floors; Furniture and Walls of Marks like Pencil Crayon; Marker; Wax Crayon; Soot; Ink; Scuffs

Shines: Jewelry; Silverware

Removes: Clothing Stains; Small Scratches and Burn Marks from Furniture and Woodwork…and much more…

OTHER HOUSEHOLD HEROES

Club Soda; Cola; Cornstarch; Dental Floss; Denture Tablets; Dishwasher Detergent; Glycerin; Hydrogen Peroxide; Lemon Juice; Lemon Oil; Linseed Oil; Mayonnaise; Milk; Mineral Oil; Petroleum Jelly; Rubber Gloves; Rubbing Alcohol…and many more!

THANKS SO MUCH TO...

Our **local and international television viewers** and **radio listeners**
who supplied us with such a variety of hints...

~ ✦ ~

The **readers** of our first two books, and our newspaper columns,
for taking the time to send us their favorite tips...

~ ✦ ~

The **companies**, **organizations** and **individuals** who provided
information and advice essential to this book...

~ ✦ ~

Our friend and partner **Margie Henderson**, who keeps all those
loose ends tied together for us...and still keeps smiling...

~ ✦ ~

Donna Dahr and her amazing test kitchen...

~ ✦ ~

Our illustrator **David McNiven**, again bringing each page to life...

~ ✦ ~

Mary Menary, for her prayers...and her garage...

~ ✦ ~

Our **family** and **friends,** for their help and encouragement...

~ ✦ ~

Our three wonderful daughters, **Erin, Kerry** and **Anna**,
for still recognizing us...

~ ✦ ~

Each other, for the constant love, and support and understanding.

TABLE OF CONTENTS

1. CLEANING 101

*"It's Easy...
If You Know How!"*

2. KLEVER KITCHEN KLEANUPS

*"Keeping Your Kitchen Spick,
Span And Spotless!"*

3. BATHROOM BEAUTIFUL

*"Cleaning...Where
You Clean Yourself!"*

4. FOILING FURNITURE FOES

*"How Not To Take
Grime Sitting Down!"*

5. REMOVING THE DIRT UNDERFOOT

*"Smart Ideas For
Carpets And Floors!"*

6. WALLS AND WINDOWS

*"Cleaning Up And
Cleaning Down!"*

7. ROUND ABOUT THE HOUSE

"The Rest Of The Nooks And Crannies!"

8. WASH-DAY WISDOM

"A Laundry List Of Smart Ideas!"

9. REGROUP AND REORGANIZE

*"Putting Clutter In Its Place,
Room By Room!"*

10. INSIDE INFO ON THE OUTSIDE

*"Cleaning Up The
Great Outdoors!"*

11. YOU AND YOURS FROM TOP TO BOTTOM

"Cleaning And Organizing...
Yourself And Your Possessions!"

12. EASY-FIND INDEX

"The Most Important Part,
Of The Book!
Find The Exact Hint
You Want Instantly!"

~ ◆ ~

CHAPTER 1

CLEANING 101

IT'S EASY…
IF YOU KNOW HOW!

ADVANCED PLANNING

CLEANING STRATEGIES...

Stay Alert For Dirt... It would amaze you at how much money is wasted by not keeping items clean. Dirty carpets last maybe half as long, clothes will wear out much quicker, walls end up having to be repainted, even light bulbs can lose up to 75% of their brightness and efficiency if they're dusty. Keep on top of your cleaning.

Tidy Before Tackling... Before you begin cleaning the items in any room, it's a good idea to tidy the room itself first. An uncluttered area is a lot easier to clean. Try it, you'll see.

Cleaning-Recipe Warning... When using homemade cleaner recipes, always read any warnings on the label of the individual ingredients that you are using in the recipe. If possible, transfer those warnings to the label on the recipe container you are filling. Play it safe and keep cleaners out of reach of children.

♦ Buy new containers to put your cleaning recipes in. Residual ingredients in used containers could react badly with whatever brand of recipe ingredient you are mixing in it.

Don't Go To Your Corner...

You'll be amazed at how many people wash themselves into a corner when cleaning floors. Plan to end up in a doorway. This way you won't track footmarks onto the damp floor.

Prevention Is Better Than Cure... The easiest way to save time cleaning up a mess or a problem is to prevent the problem in the first place. For example, placing a really good absorbent floor mat inside the front door saves a lot of floor cleanup. Before you bake a casserole in the oven, place the casserole dish in a pan of water. Any spills will end up in the water and not on your oven floor. See the oven-cleaning time you just saved?

A Gem Of A Tip... If you value your jewelry, you should always remove your rings when you wash dishes. But why not pop them into some jewelry cleaner at the same time? Saves you taking time out to clean them!

Dishwasher Time-Saver...

When loading the cutlery basket in your dishwasher, it's a good idea to give each of the basket's compartments its own item ...like spoons in one, forks in another, etc. This will save you time when transferring the cleaned cutlery to your cutlery drawer compartments.

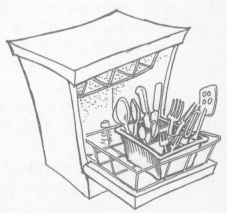

Cook-Time Cleaning... It's a good idea to use your cooking time to clean out the fridge. You're going into it anyway to get ingredients, so why not tackle two jobs with one effort!

♦ When preparing a meal, fill your kitchen sink with hot sudsy water. This way you can pop the used pots and dishware into the water and let them soak while you cook. Cleanup will be a lot quicker and easier because of the soaking they got.

Separate Cloths... Avoid having to constantly rinse out your cleaning cloth by preparing a separate cloth, sponge or brush for each type of cleaner—e.g., mirrors and windows, wooden floors, tile floors, furniture, counters, sinks, etc. In this case, less isn't more.

Buy The Economy Size... You can save a fortune by buying the large economy-size containers of versatile cleaning materials like vinegar, baking soda, water-less hand cleaner, etc. Not only is it cheaper to buy in bulk, but you'll also save a lot of time-wasting trips to the store. As a bonus, by decanting each large container into several smaller contain-ers, you have the convenience of having accessible containers of cleaning materials in different rooms.

Plan To Get The Kids Involved... Give the kids some thick soft socks to put over their hands and let them dust the furniture for you.

♦ Look for a brightly colored feather duster the next time you're at the store. Most kids love to dust with a feather duster.

Exercleaning... Put an up-tempo tape or CD in your stereo or walkman. Not only will it distract you from the drudgery and make the time fly, chances are you could lose a few calories in the process.

YOUR CLEANING CREDO

CLEANING PHILOSOPHY...

Save Effort... If it is already clean...then don't clean it. You'd be surprised at how much time is wasted by cleaning items that don't need to be cleaned, just because they happen to be in your line of momentum!

Save Money... Always use cleaning cloths, sponges and brushes instead of disposable cloths and paper towels. Your pocket (and environment) will thank you for it!

♦ Often less is more. For example, a long stream of dish soap in your sink water will not get your dishes any cleaner than a short squirt. You can apply this same rule of thumb to hair shampoo and many other cleaners.

♦ Let items soak longer. You'll find that you use less detergent that way.

The 5-Minute Cleanup... Save staring an ominous cleaning task in the face by doing a daily 5-minute collection of all those things lying around. Put them in their rightful place and believe me, you'll make your regular cleaning day much easier and you, much happier.

The 10-Minute Cleanup... Clean a different part of your house each day for just 10 minutes—that's all. You'll be surprised at how little you'll have to clean by the week's end.

Don't Put It Down Until Later... Take the time to drop off that item you're holding in it's rightful place. Don't take the chance of cluttering up your home by leaving it somewhere it doesn't belong until later. Usually "later" never comes!

Take It With You... If you're going from one room to another, make a habit of picking up something that belongs in the room you're heading for.

Less Is More (Space)... Chances are you don't really need two drawers full of plastic containers. Cut down on clutter by keeping only the amount of containers you know you'll use.

Dust Direction... When dusting, start at the top and work your way down (exactly opposite to your career!). Let gravity work **for** you rather than against you.

Ruthless Rules… In order to avoid house clutter you have to follow these five ruthless rules. Get rid of it, if:
♦ you haven't touched it in the last year or two.
♦ it's not worth storing in your own home.
♦ it's broken and really not worth getting repaired.
♦ you **want** it more than you need it.
♦ it's easily replaced.

TOOLS OF THE TRADE

DUST BUSTERS…

Dust Removers… A paper or plastic bag comes in handy for "pollution-wise" mop cleaning. Here's how. Place a plastic or paper bag over the mop head and secure with a twist tie or rubber band. Shake vigorously and discard the bag filled with dust. This trick is especially useful for apartment dwellers.

Dust Detractors… Fabric-softener sheets are great for cleaning eyeglasses. It also helps prevent them fogging up. Use them also for keeping dust off your TV and monitor screens.

Dust Attractors… For a cheap and convenient dusting tool, wet two socks and place one on each hand. Two-fisted dusting in half the time!

Brief Duster... Men's old cotton underwear makes a great lint-free dust cloth.

Fridge Dust Bunnies... The brush on the other end of the handle of your car's ice scraper is just the right size for getting at the dust and dirt that collects under your refrigerator. Its also great for dusting the coils on the back of your fridge.

♦ Or take a yardstick and place an old sock over the end. Tape it on with some duct tape and dust to your heart's content.

Awkward Areas... For dusty places that are difficult to reach with regular cleaning rags, try using a soft-bristled paintbrush instead. Choose the right size for the job and brush away.

♦ The small sponge paintbrushes are also good for cleaning. Not only can they access tight areas, but they hold soap and water well too.

High-Up Areas... For cleaning dust and spider webs from ceilings, etc., a great idea is to recycle your old telescoping golf-ball retriever. Just pop a sponge over the end, slip an old sock over the sponge and secure it with a rubber band.

Dustpans... Sprinkle a little water on your dustpan just before using it. It'll help prevent the dust and sweepings from falling out.

♦ Did you know a rubber dustpan is handy for picking up wet spills? Try it!

Brush Bonanza... An old shaving brush is great for dusting. Its soft bristles are ideal for "sensitive" surfaces like antiques.

♦ A great device for cleaning hard to reach areas, like inside lidless kettles, thermos flasks, etc., is a baby-bottle brush.

Snow "Removal"... A clever way to clean your broom in the winter is to take it outside and sweep it through a snow-bank a few times!

CLEVER CLEANERS...

The Button Scraper... Here's a clever idea for your washup cloths. Sew a large plastic or wooden button onto the one corner of the cloth. It makes a great scraper for those hard-to-remove pieces of food on dishes and pots, etc. And it won't harm most surfaces either.

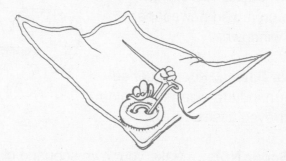

Back Saver... When scrubbing hard-to-reach areas, try using a toilet brush. You'll find the extra length will really help your back.

Rinse Aid... Buy an extra, inexpensive plastic watering can next time you're in a garden store. Its makes rinsing your bathtub a lot easier.

No-Plunger Plumbing... If you find yourself with a plugged sink drain and no plunger, use a Frisbee. Fill your sink with hot water, place the Frisbee over the drain hole and pump it hard several times. It often works surprisingly well!

The Final Shine... Bring a gleam to your shoes with a piece of that leftover plush carpeting. Cut a piece and simply glue it to a small block of wood.

♦ Stop! Don't throw away those old shoulder pads from your cast-off blouses and dresses. They make great, soft, easy-grip furniture or shoe-polishing tools. Try them, you'll see!

♦ Old oven-mitt liners and sweatpants pockets make great cleaning mitts.

Save On Paper Toweling... Use crumpled newspaper to dry windows.

Friendly Filter... Keep a coffee filter handy to clean and shine your eyeglasses.

On A Scour Note... Make your own scouring cleaner by sprinkling salt on the surface to be cleaned and rubbing it with a cloth dipped in lemon juice or distilled white vinegar.

Dental Cleaning... Keep a small toothbrush handy to remove foods from your grater. The bristles are just the right size and stiffness for the job.

♦ A piece of dental floss comes in handy for cleaning between the blades of awkward utensils such as pizza cutters and can openers.

The Gentle Scraper... To make a great scraper that is strong but won't damage the surface of your pots and pans, take a wooden spoon and a handsaw. Square off the rounded end by cutting off half the spoon's bowl and sand the edge smooth.

♦ A rubber spatula works well for scraping food off dishes. It's really gentle.

♦ An expired plastic membership card works really well to remove hardened buildup on your sensitive pots and pans.

Dishwasher... Take a small baby-food bottle and poke a few holes through the lid. Then cut a piece of sponge (cellulose is best) to the size and shape of  the lid and glue it onto the top of the lid. Fill the bottle with dish soap and screw on the "sponge-lid" for a great, easy-grip dishwasher!

All-Purpose Cleaner... Citrus fruits like lemons, oranges and limes, when freshly squeezed, make good all-purpose cleaners. Simply mix the juice with water for day-to-day regular cleaning, but for stubborn stains, use full strength.

Baby Yourself... It's a good idea to keep a few baby wipes on hand even if you don't have a baby. They're great for removing those unexpected spills and stains from clothing.

Window Wiper... A recycled car window wiper makes a great squeegee for cleaning linoleum and vinyl floors. Attach it to a broom handle to avoid bending over. Works on windows too, of course.

Panty Hose Brings A Twinkle To Your Eye... Don't throw out that old panty hose. They're great for bringing that extra gleam to your floors when you use them as buffing cloths.

Terry-Towel Tip... Recycle those old terry bath and swim towels. Cut them into usable sizes and hem the edges. Great wash and buff rags!

Pumice Anyone?... A pumice stone is really handy for removing those hard watermarks from your bathtub, sinks and toilets. Make sure you buy the right kind for the surface you are working on.

Cleaner Tote... A plastic bathroom caddy makes a convenient carrier for many of your cleaning tools and containers.

♦ Recycle your child's nylon school lunch bag as a cleaner tote. The nylon is strong and many of them have outside web pockets that are ideal for holding damp sponges and wipes. They have convenient handles too.

Garbage Apron... A quick and effective apron to protect your clothes when scrubbing is an ordinary plastic garbage bag. Simply cut out holes for your head and arms.

~ ♦ ~

CHAPTER 2

KLEVER KITCHEN KLEANUPS

KEEPING YOUR KITCHEN
SPICK, SPAN AND SPOTLESS!

APPLIANCES...
BIGGER THAN
A BREAD BOX

Whiter-Than-White Appliances... Keep white appliances sparkling clean and prevent yellowing by washing with a mixture of ½ cup of bleach, 8 cups of water and ½ cup of baking soda. Rinse well with clean water and dry thoroughly. Then rinse again with 1 cup of vinegar and 1 teaspoon. lemon juice. Buff to shine. *Caution: Do not use this method on stainless-steel appliances. Do not mix vinegar with bleach.*

Stainless, Stainless Steel... To remove those unsightly finger marks from your stainless-steel appliances, try wiping the surface down with baby oil. Rinse off with club soda.

FRIDGES AND FREEZERS...

A Fresh Fridge... Freshen up the inside of your refrigerator by wiping periodically with a cloth moistened with vinegar. It's also a great way to prevent that mildew buildup.

♦ A weak solution of ordinary club soda and a little salt can also get your fridge fresh. Simply apply with a soft cloth.

♦ For a more challenging cleaning job, wipe down the interior with a solution of 3 tablespoons baking soda in 4 cups of warm water. If you encounter any hard-to-remove deposits, apply a thick paste of water and baking soda, let it sit for an hour or two and rinse off with a white vinegar and water solution.

♦ Keep an open box of baking soda in your fridge at all times. Replace the box every 3 months. But don't waste the old box of baking soda. Use it for other cleaning purposes.

♦ Or leave a cotton ball soaked with peppermint extract on a small plate inside the fridge.

♦ Line part of your fridge shelves with plastic place mats. This way, if there are any spills, it contains them to the mat, which is a lot easier cleaned than all the shelves beneath it!

A Fresh Freezer...
One way to get rid of freezer odor is with ordinary fresh bread. Just place a loaf or two in your freezer and leave for about 3 or 4 nights. Should do the trick!

♦ Line the floor of your freezer compartment with aluminum foil. If any frozen foods leak before they're frozen, this will prevent them sticking to the freezer floor and, as a result, save you a messy and lengthy cleanup job.

STOVES, OVENS AND MICROWAVES...

Stove-Top Cleaning... Most stove tops can be washed down with hot water and regular detergent. However, for those hard-to-remove spills, both on the range surface and the chrome and stainless-steel parts, use a little baking soda and water. Simply apply a smooth paste to the area, leave for 5 to 10 minutes and then wipe off with a soft cloth. Rinse with a white vinegar and water solution.

♦ Another good way to get your oven top clean is to mix equal parts warm water and ammonia. Apply, wait 30 seconds and then rub as necessary.

♦ Rubbing alcohol can also bring a beautiful shine to your stove top.

♦ To clean and shine those messy chrome burner trim rings, rub well with a paste of vinegar and cream of tartar.

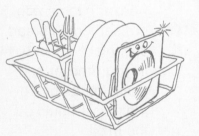

Stove-Burner Drip Pans... For a quick way to clean burner drip pans and rings, simply add them to your next dishwasher cycle.

♦ For stubborn stains on drip trays, place an ammonia-soaked cloth in it and leave it overnight. Wash off well with dish soap and water.

 **Hot Tips For Oven Spills...** When oven spills occur, sprinkle with a mixture of one part cinnamon and six parts table salt. When the oven is cool, wipe up the mixture. Not only will it absorb the spill but it'll help remove the burned food odor.

♦ To dislodge baked-on spills, apply a paste of baking soda (or borax) and water. Sometimes a little elbow grease is necessary!

♦ Or for stubborn deposits, place a shallow oven-safe dish of ammonia on the upper rack and a pan of water on the lower rack of a still-hot oven. Leave overnight. Air oven and wipe grease away with an all-purpose cleaner and some warm water. An inexpensive way of oven cleaning.

Oven Racks... Place your oven racks in a garbage bag and throw in an ammonia-soaked cloth. Seal tightly and leave outside overnight. Wash down well with soap and water the next day.

Oven Trays... Prevention is better than cure. Add a small amount of water to your trays when baking or broiling. This could save you a lot of time when it comes to cleaning them.

♦ Or simply cover the bottom of the pan with aluminum foil. This works for the bottom of your oven too, by the way.

♦ Oven trays and pans should be dried well after washing to prevent rusting. Pop them in a warm oven to dry them really well.

Oven Window… To tackle that brown-stained oven window, make a thick paste of water and baking soda. Simply coat the inside of the window well with the mixture, leave on for 10 to 15 minutes or until completely dry and then scour off with clean water.

A Fresh Microwave… To freshen up and deodorize your microwave oven, place a heat-resistant bowl of water on the carousel and add 3 or 4 slices of lemon. Cook it on high for about 30 seconds.

♦ Another great microwave freshener is to add several drops of vanilla extract to a small heat-resistant bowl of water. Place it in the center of your microwave and heat for 30 seconds or so.

Getting Your Microwave Clean… A quick way to clean and deodorize your microwave is to put a small, heat-resistant container in the center of the microwave and fill it with white vinegar. Heat the vinegar and let it boil for a minute or so. Using rubber gloves (it'll be really hot), wipe down with a soft cloth dipped into the hot vinegar.

Keeping Your Microwave Clean… Remember to always place a lid of some sort on the container (not metal) when cooking. This helps prevent those messy food spatters on the inside.

♦ Also, it's a good idea to cover the carousel tray with wax wrap. Put a fresh piece on every so often and you'll hardly ever have to clean it!

DISHWASHER DOS AND DON'TS…

Removing Dishwasher Film… The inside of your dishwasher will be film free if you do this occasionally. Fill washer with dirty dishes, but make sure you have not included any silver or other metals. Place a shallow bowl with ½ cup of bleach on the bottom rack and allow the machine to run through the wash cycle only. Fill the same bowl with ½ cup of vinegar and this time allow the machine to run through a full cycle.

Removing Dishwasher Stains… A quick way to get rid of those yellow stains in your dishwasher is to first allow your empty machine to fill for a wash. Then add a package of flavored orange or lemon crystals (the kind you make drinks out of) and allow the wash and rinse cycle to complete.

♦ Or rub the dishwasher's interior down with mineral oil. Then run it through a full cycle with regular dishwasher soap.

♦ Baking soda can also do the trick. Rub with a damp cloth and then run through a cycle with regular dishwasher soap.

♦ Sometimes discoloration marks can be prevented by switching from liquid dishwasher detergent to the powdered variety.

Dishwasher Odor… Offensive dishwasher odors can often be removed by simply running the wash cycle for 30 seconds to add water to the bottom of the washer. Then pour in 1 cup of baking soda and let stand overnight. Restart the cycle in the morning.

Dishwasher Spots… Here's an inexpensive alternative to those commercial dishwasher-spot removers for glassware and dishware…ordinary distilled white vinegar.

APPLIANCES… SMALLER THAN A BREAD BOX

TOASTERS, KETTLES AND ALL THEIR FRIENDS…

Toaster Trick… When you have a toaster on the counter, you usually have a bread bag nearby. This often means that you end up with a piece of the plastic bag melted on the side of the toaster. Well, it can be removed easily with a little nail-polish remover or acetone on a soft cloth. It'll also bring a nice shine to the chrome. Keep the remover away from plastic parts on the toaster though, it can mar their surface.

 Kettle Kleaners… A great way to descale your kettle is to place two tablespoons of water softener in the kettle. Top it up with water and let it boil for a few minutes. Repeat if necessary.

♦ Or clean your kettle periodically by boiling equal parts vinegar and water in it. Let it sit overnight and rinse it well in the morning. The lime deposits should wash away.

♦ Want a quick and easy way to bring a shine to your kettle's exterior? Try buffing it with a piece of waxed paper! Make sure it's not hot though!

Aluminum Percolators... It's not a good idea to use bleach to clean your aluminum percolator (or anything aluminum for that matter). Instead, fill it up with water and add about a quarter cup of cream of tartar. Run it through a cycle and then rinse well with hot water.

Coffeemakers... Give your coffeemaker a treat every so often. Clean it by filling the reservoir with water and adding two tablespoons of water softener. Run the machine through its cycle once, then again with plain water.

♦ Or fill the reservoir with white vinegar and run it through a full cycle. Repeat the cycle twice with plain water.

♦ Another good cleaning method is to fill the reservoir with hot water and add a regular denture tablet to it. Run the machine through a cycle and repeat with clean water.

Overflowing Coffeemakers... Often coffeemakers overflow due to the filter not sitting properly in the basket. To save wiping up those spills, simply wet the filter a little before placing it in the basket. This will usually hold it in place through the cycle.

Blender Cleaning... Add ½ teaspoon dish soap to your blender. Fill halfway with hot tap water, turn it on high and blend it clean. The blades create a soapy water vortex that cleans most buildup really quickly.

Messy Mixers?... Use a little glycerin or vegetable oil to lubricate egg beaters. It'll make for a much easier cleanup.

Can-Opener Groomer!... Remove food buildup from under the blades of your manual and electric can openers with the brush you get with an electric shaver. It's just the right size and firm enough to access those awkward spots.

Garbage Disposer... To clean your garbage disposer easily, simply cut a lemon in quarters and drop the pieces into the hole. You'll find this will not only clean the blades, but it will also add a nice fresh lemony fragrance to your disposer.

♦ For garbage-disposer odor, try adding 2 or 3 tablespoons of pure vanilla essence.

But What *About* The Bread Box?... To help keep your bread from going moldy too quickly, place a box of blackboard chalk in the bread box. It'll keep the air drier inside.

POTS, PANS AND PARAPHERNALIA

POTS AND PANS...

Pots... Try removing stubborn food residue from pots (not aluminum) with this trick. Pour in a small amount of bleach and add some hot water. Let the solution sit in the pot 3 to 4 hours (or overnight) and it should come clean effortlessly. Rinse well with clean water and dish detergent.

♦ To remove residue from aluminum pots, pour in a half cup of white vinegar and a half cup of hot water and let the pot soak for 2 to 3 hours. Wash out with regular dish soap and water.

Nonstick Pots And Pans... To remove stains on nonstick finishes, mix 2 tablespoons baking powder, ½ cup chlorine bleach and 1 cup of water. Put the mixture in the stained pot and let it boil for about 10 minutes. Wash with soap and water, dry, then rub a little vegetable oil on the surface. Don't allow the mixture to boil over or it might leave spots on the exterior finish of the pot. Also, don't use this method on aluminum pots or pans.

Nonimmersible Pots And Pans... To clean your electric cookware that can't be immersed in water, simply fill it half full of water, add a little dish soap and set it to a medium heat for about a half hour. For stubborn dirt, add 2 table-spoons water softener to the water. Keep an eye on it to check that the water does not boil away.

Pans... For an effortless way to remove caked-on food from pans and baking sheets, pour in a little hot water and throw in a denture tablet. Leave overnight and wipe off the next day.

Saving Scorched Pans... Remove as much burned food as possible from the pan with a plastic or wooden utensil. Sprinkle the bottom with baking soda to form a good layer over the burned area. Add 1½ cups water and let it stand overnight. Use the same plastic or wooden utensil to scrape and lift the remains. Scour if necessary. Do not use this method on aluminum pans.

♦ Another way to loosen baked-on food from the inside of your pots and pans is to coat the surface with dish-washer liquid and leave for a few hours. Remove the remains as above.

♦ A great all-purpose abrasive cleaner for pots and pans is a mixture of one part baking soda and two parts borax. Store it in a container with holes in the lid to create your own shaker and keep it handy in your kitchen.

Aluminum Pots And Pans... To remove discoloration from your aluminum pots and pans, try this. Mix 2 tablespoons white vinegar with 1½ tablespoons cream of tartar and add it to the pot with 4 cups of water. Continue heating until the pot or pan is clean.

Copper-Bottom Cleaning...
A little salt and vinegar or salt and lemon juice will clean copper bottoms on pots and pans. Just sprinkle on, rub lightly and wash as usual. Just remember, this may  make them look nice, but the duller the copper bottom on your pot, the better the heat transference.

Enamelware... Often you can remove small rust marks from your enamel pots and pans by rubbing with a little baking powder on a damp cloth.

Cleaning Enamel Broiling Pans... Remove tough-to-clean food and grease from broiling pans by covering the bottom with a ¼-inch layer of water softener. Place a wet terry or dish towel over the area and leave for several hours. This should loosen baked-on grease enough to wash it off without a lot of effort.

Cast-Iron Cookware... To clean the INSIDE of your cast-iron cookware, instead of washing after each use try shaking salt onto the cookware and wiping it clean. This keeps food from sticking when frying and needs only to be washed every other use. A light coating of cooking oil every so often won't hurt either. Helps prevents rust!

♦ To clean the OUTSIDE of your cast-iron pan, simply give it a wipe with a sheet of waxed paper while it's still a little warm.

PARAPHERNALIA...

Wok Cleaning... A well-seasoned wok should require only a quick rub down with a damp cloth to remove surface deposits. Follow up with a wipe from a cloth dipped in vegetable oil.

Glass Baking Dishes... Baking soda on a damp rag will usually do a good cleaning job on glass baking dishes, but for more stubborn residue you can try scouring them with a little salt on a damp cloth. Rinse well with clean water.

♦ Or pour in a solution of eight parts hot water to one part dishwasher soap Let it soak overnight and then rinse out with clean water.

Ceramic Bakeware... Treat the same as for glass baking dishes.

Rusty Baking Dishes... Believe it or not, rust can often be removed from metal baking dishes by scouring them well with half of a raw potato and your favorite powdered detergent.

♦ For an effortless method of cleaning off those rust marks, simply pour a little cola in the dish and soak it overnight.

Six-Second Silver Cleaning... Run about a quart of hot water into your kitchen or bathroom sink (cool enough not to burn you). Dissolve 1 tablespoon water softener (or laundry washing soda*) and 1 tablespoon salt in the water. Place a sheet of aluminum foil on the bottom of the sink and place your tarnished silver on the foil.** The silver that's both touching the foil and covered by the water should become clean within 10 seconds. If the piece is badly tarnished, rub it with a soft cloth after removing it from the water.

*Important: Outside North America, see "washing soda" reference in the glossary of terms at the back of this book.
*Do not ues this method when silver has been antiqued.

♦ This method works on silver and gold jewelry too. But don't use it on jewelry that has been set with stones. It could loosen the settings and damage the stones.

♦ Or you can mix some lemon juice and salt, dip a soft cloth in it and rub your silver with it. Rinse off with clean water and dry well.

Clever Cutlery Cleaning... Remove stubborn egg stains on flatware by rubbing with a mixture of table salt and tomato juice.

♦ To remove fingerprints from your stainless-steel cutlery, simply rub with a cloth dampened with white vinegar.

Collective Cutlery Cleaning!... Want a time-saver? When 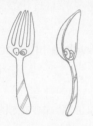 washing a lot of cutlery by hand, pop a colander into the soapy wash water. As you wash, place the cutlery into the colander. Now you can rinse all the cutlery at the same time by running the full colander under the cold-water tap.

♦ Make sure you don't mix cutlery of different metals in the dishwasher basket. If they touch each other, they can cause discoloration.

Spick-And-Span Sponges... A great way to clean and freshen your cleaning sponges is to soak them every so often in salt water. Rinse out with clean water afterward.

♦ A quick an easy way to remove bacteria buildup on your sponges and dishcloths is to zap them in the microwave for half a minute. But remember to be careful when removing them…they'll be HOT! HOT! HOT!

No-Clean Containers… When measuring gooey ingredients like honey, butter or margarine, line the container with a sheet of plastic  shrink-wrap first. Remove the wrap once the measuring is done and you have no container to clean!

Preventing Plastic-Container Stains… To prevent tomato-based foods from staining your plastic containers, soak the container and lid in cold water for 5 minutes or so before filling.

♦ Or wipe the inside of the container with a little cooking oil.

Removing Plastic-Container Stains… Usually most stains can be removed, or at the very least faded, by placing the open container outside in direct sunlight for a period of time.

And Eliminating Their Odors!… A method that many people use is to wash the container with soap and water and place it open in the freezer for 48 hours.

♦ Eliminate odors in plastic containers by placing ordinary newspaper, crumpled into several balls, inside the container before securing the lid. Odors should be gone overnight. Wash out well with dish soap and water.

♦ You can also rub the inside down with a little tomato juice. Leave for an hour or so and rinse off with soap and water.

♦ Freshen up your child's lunch bag or lunch box by placing a piece of white bread soaked in distilled white vinegar inside. Leave the bag to sit for an hour or two.

Wooden Cutting Boards… Slice a lemon or lime and rub the board vigorously. Rinse with cold water. Clean and fresh smelling too!

♦ Or, rub down with ammonia and baking soda. Make sure you rinse it very well with water and white vinegar afterward.

♦ Treat unfinished boards with a coating of mineral oil once a year. Do the same to season your unfinished wooden bowls.

A Grateful Grater!… Rub a small amount of vegetable oil or margarine on the grater before using it. Cleaning up will be a lot quicker.

Bright Thermos Tips… Freshen up thermos bottles or insulated coffeepots by filing with warm water mixed with 2 tablespoons of water softener. Leave to soak a while and wash out well with clean water afterward. You won't believe the results!

♦ For more stubborn stains, add some raw rice to the bottom of your thermos with some  soapy water and baking soda. Shake the thermos gently and rinse with clean water.

Thermos Odor... To deodorize your thermos flask and other closed jugs, etc., simply pour in a ¼ cup of salt and let it sit for a day or two. Rinse with clean water.

Pot Holders... Spray your pot holders with spray starch to help prevent those grease stains. Reapply after each wash.

THE DIRT ON DISHWARE

DISHES, CUPS, ETC....

Washing Dishes... If your dishes have that greasy buildup and you're washing them by hand, simply toss a half cup of ordinary baking soda into the dishwater along with the dishes. You should find it cuts the dishwater grease considerably.

♦ Vinegar is also a good thing to add to your dishwashing water. It's a mild grease cutter and also a mild disinfectant.

♦ A good rule is to start with the cleanest dishes and work your way up to the dirtiest ones. This way you won't have to change the dishwater nearly as often.

♦ If you get your children to do the dishes (as you should), you may find they're not as gentle with them as you would be. You may want to consider buying your dishes from a restaurant-supply store. They're likely to be much more kid resistant!

Dish Washing Soap... Save money and recycle at the same time, by collecting all your bath soap slivers and grating them into a container. Add 1 or 2 tablespoons baking soda and boiling water. Decant the mixture into an empty dish soap bottle and voilà...homemade dish detergent!

Dishwasher Direction... To get the most out of your dishwasher, remember to place your dishware facing into the direction of the spray and place all your cups facing mouth down.

Casserole And Baking Dishes... Top up your grimy casserole or baking dish with hot water and add a half cup of automatic dishwasher detergent (liquid or powder). Leave it to soak for a few hours and it should rinse clean easily.

♦ Or sprinkle about 5 or 6 tablespoons borax onto the bottom of the dish, add 1 teaspoon dish soap and top up with hot water. Leave for 30 minutes and rinse off with clean water.

Delicate China... For china cups that have become stained, pop in a denture tablet and top the cup up with warm water. Leave to sit for an hour or so and rinse with clean water.

Removing Scratches... To remove black cutlery marks from the glazed surface of your fine china plates, try this little trick. Apply some ordinary white toothpaste to a clean soft cloth and rub the marks gently. Rinse off with water.

Tea And Coffee Stains... These stains can be removed safely from teacups and coffee cups, and even your fine china, by rubbing gently with a cloth sprinkled with baking soda.

♦ Or you can use water softener the same way. It works great too!

♦ Stubborn tea and coffee stains can also be removed from cups and china teapots by making a solution of 1 tablespoon chlorine bleach and 1 quart warm water. Let the solution sit in them for an hour or so. Wash well with dish soap and rinse really well afterward with clean water.

GETTING YOUR GLASSWARE GLEAMING

REGULAR GLASSWARE...

Keep Off The Glass... Stubborn stains and discoloration on your glassware can sometimes be removed by soaking the item in a solution of one part salt and eight parts white vinegar.

♦ You can also soak the glass in ammonia for an hour or so. Rinse really well afterward.

♦ Or try a solution of 2 tablespoons water softener and warm water.

♦ For a more stubborn film or even light scratches, buy some iron oxide, sometimes called jeweler's polishing rouge, from your jeweler. Mix equal parts oxide, glycerin and water and apply the paste to the area with a cloth. Rinse off well with dish soap and warm water.

♦ Believe it or not, sometimes that white film can be removed by laying wet potato peels on the stained area overnight. Rinse the next day with clean warm water.

Mega Glass Cleaning... Just had a large party
and lots of glasses to clean? Well, do what
many banquet companies do. Fill your sink
with water as hot as the glass will stand and
add your dish soap. Fill the other sink (or a
pail if you have only one sink) with hot water only. Using
rubber dishwashing gloves, hold each glass, mouth down,
and plunge it up and down several times in the soapy
water. Then repeat the process in the clear water immediately. Believe me, you'll find this is a much easier way of
getting through all those dirty glasses in a hurry.

DELICATE GLASSWARE...

Crystal Care... Remember to never wash lead crystal pieces
in very hot water and certainly not in the dishwasher.

Crystal Clear!... Vinegar cleans crystal beautifully. Wash in a
mixture of 1 cup distilled white vinegar and 3 cups warm
water. Allow to air-dry.

Delicate Glassware... Always
slip delicate glassware into
hot water on it's side. Its
also a good idea to line
the bottom of the sink with
a soft terry towel to protect
your glassware.

♦ Don't use a regular kitchen brush to clean out the
patterned surface of cut-glass pieces. Try an electric-
razor brush instead. It's firm but gentle bristles are just
right for getting into those really intricate glass
patterns.

Stemware… It's really not a good idea to wash your stemware in the dishwasher. Play it safe and wash it by hand instead.

Removing Labels… For those "immovable" labels and the residue they leave on glassware and jars, try soaking a cloth in warm, white vinegar and laying it over the label for about 15 minutes or so. It should come off fairly easily.

COUNTERS, CUPBOARDS …
AND THE KITCHEN SINK

COUNTERS…

NB: It's always a good idea to check manufacturer's recommendations before using any cleaners on your kitchen counters. With the wide variety of materials used nowadays, surfaces can react differently to certain cleaning solutions.

Counter Cleaner… Fill a spray bottle with equal parts water, white vinegar and add a teaspoon of salt. Shake well to dissolve the salt. You can also substitute lemon juice for the vinegar.

♦ A paste of baking soda and water (or lemon juice) works too. Rub, leave for 15 minutes and then rinse off.

◆ Or mix 2 tablespoons white vinegar, 2 tablespoons ammonia and 1 cup of warm water. Wipe or sponge the solution on and rinse off.

Counter Marks… Stick several of those furniture floor-scuff pads under your counter appliances. This will help prevent scuff marks and scratches on your counter surface. If you don't have any scuff pads, corn plasters work well too!

Counter Crumbs… Place your toaster on a small attractive metal tray. This will contain all those crumbs that usually spread over the counter and end up having to be cleaned off the floor.

Bacteria Prevention… Wipe up leftover blood and meat juice from your counter using a paper towel and discard it immediately. Then wipe down the counter with distilled white vinegar.

Degreasing Cupboards… To remove the greasy buildup on your kitchen cupboards, make a thick paste of baking soda and water. Wipe it on the surface and let it sit until it's completely dry. Remove as much baking-soda residue as you can and then give your cupboards a good wipe down with a little white vinegar. Rinse with clean, warm water.

◆ Inside shelves can be wiped down with a damp cloth dipped in baking soda. Repeat with a cloth dipped in vinegar.

 **Cupboard Mold…** If you use water to wipe your shelves down, make sure you dry the shelves well, otherwise mold can form in the crevices…and you wouldn't want that!

Cupboard Stains… Most common stains can be removed from painted kitchen cupboard doors and surfaces by simply rubbing with a soft cloth and a little ordinary dish soap.

♦ For stubborn stains, however, make up a solution of 2 tablespoons of lemon oil, 1 teaspoon of turpentine and 2 cups of hot water. Wipe on and rinse off with a clean damp cloth.

Cupboard Odor… Every so often give the inside of your cupboards a treat. Wipe them down with some distilled white vinegar. This will not only help keep any of those musty odors at bay, but it'll disinfect the inside at the same time.

♦ It's a good idea to store your glasses upright on your cupboard shelves. If they're stored mouth down they tend to take on the odor of the material the shelf is made of.

SINKS…

Cleaning Stainless-Steel Sinks… Want to give your stainless-steel kitchen sink a good clean? All you really need is some baking soda. Sprinkle a little on a wet cloth or sponge and wipe the sink with it. Buff with a paper towel afterward.

♦ Rubbing alcohol is good for removing those stubborn water spots. Rinse off afterward with club soda or white vinegar.

♦ If the problem is streak marks on your stainless steel, wipe them down with a little baby oil or even a little lemon oil.

Rust Marks… Sometimes rust marks form on stainless-steel sinks. They can often be removed by rubbing the area with a little lighter fluid. Be careful, it's very flammable.

Sink Brighteners… After cleaning your stainless-steel sink with your Haley's Hint, you can bring a brilliant shine to it by buffing with either distilled white vinegar or a little ammonia on a paper towel.

Sink Conservation Tip… When washing dishes in a double sink, run hot water into the second sink. Use this to rinse the dishes in, instead of running the water constantly. It's quicker, smarter and water conservative. Of course, if you don't have a second sink, use a plastic bucket or large plastic basin instead.

Stopper Cleaning… For an easy way to keep your sink stoppers squeaky clean, include them in the basket along with your cutlery when you run your dishwasher.

Leak Prevention… When soaking items for a long time in your sink, prevent the water leaking past the stopper and emptying your sink by wrapping the stopper in plastic shrink-wrap.

Plugged Drain... Pour about 5 or 6 tablespoons baking soda down the drain.
  Immediately add a cup of vinegar and,
  once the fizzing and bubbling stops,
  follow with a kettle of boiling water.

Drain Maintenance... Every month or so,
  give your sink drain a perk up. Pour a
  ½ cup of salt down the sink drain and
  follow it with a kettle of boiling water. This should prevent
  most grease buildup and deodorize it at the same time.

AND DON'T FORGET

CLEANING AND DEODORIZING ETC....

Kitchen Table Cleaning... To get your arborite kitchen tabletop beautifully clean with no streaks, wipe the surface with
  a mixture of 3 tablespoons distilled white vinegar, 1 teaspoon rubbing alcohol and ⅔ cup of water. Add a few drops
  of lemon extract to your new table cleaner for a nice fresh
  fragrance.

Fruit And Veggie Cleaning...
A good way to clean your fruit
and vegetables really well is to
rinse them with a combination of
half distilled white vinegar and
half cold water.

♦ If you're concerned about there being some crawly critters still on the veggies, then fill your sink with cold water, mix in ¼ cup salt and soak the veggies in it. Any unwanted guests will usually die and end up on the surface of the water, where they can be skimmed off easily.

Clam Cleaning... You're gonna love this one. When soaking clams, add a ¼ cup of cornmeal to the water. The irritated clams should get rid of any sand or grit along with the cornmeal!

Dishwasher No-No... It's probably not a good idea to put the following items in your dishwasher. But check your particular dishwasher's instruction manual first to make sure:
Cast iron
Anodized aluminum
Pewter
Antique or hand-painted china
China or crystal with gold or platinum edging
Wooden utensils
Heat-sensitive plastics

Onion Hands... Believe it or not, you can usually remove most of the onion smell from your hands after cutting onions by simply taking hold of a stainless-steel spoon and running that hand under the cold-water tap for about 30 seconds. The smell will vanish miraculously. They actually sell a stainless-steel gadget in the stores that does the same thing, but why pay for it when you don't have to?

♦ If you don't believe the previous hint, you can try rubbing them with salt and vinegar...your hands that is, not the onions!

Garlic Odor... When you're cooking a recipe that requires a lot of garlic in it, you may want to boil some distilled white vinegar in a container on the stove at the same time. It should help cut down on the garlic smell considerably.

~ ♦ ~

CHAPTER 3

BATHROOM BEAUTIFUL

CLEANING...
WHERE YOU CLEAN YOURSELF!

TUB TRICKS AND SINK SECRETS

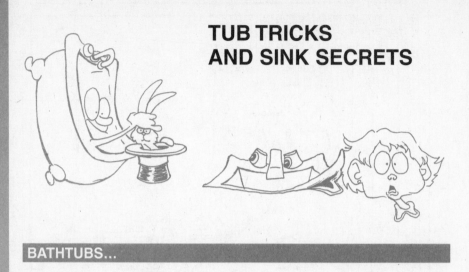

BATHTUBS...

Wet 'N' Dry... A good daily habit to get into is to rinse the bathtub as soon as you're finished and dry it immediately. This will help prevent you having to scrub off all those stubborn watermarks and soap film that have had a chance to set.

Ring Around The Bathtub... For an effortless way to prevent bathtub rings simply use a little nonoily bubble bath.

♦ If you don't have any bubble bath, you can always use a little hair shampoo.

♦ To remove those stubborn tub rings, you can also wash with vinegar or a warm solution of water softener and water.

♦ Or mix a paste of borax and lemon juice and scrub well. Let it dry and rinse off. This works for cleaning tiled and acrylic shower walls too.

Let It Soak… As soon as the kids are out of the bath, apply your cleaner to the tub and leave it. By the time you've put the kids' jammies on, tucked them into their little beds and read them a story, the cleaner will have had time to loosen all that grime and make your cleanup job a lot easier.

Timely Tools… Keep an extra toilet brush in the bathroom and use it to clean your bathtub with. The firm bristles are great for cleaning, but think also of how it'll save your back!

Baby Bath Time… Scrub your baby's bath with a little baking soda, rather than a harsh chemical cleaning detergent.

Acrylic Bath Time… Remember, it makes sense never to use any harsh, abrasive cleansers or scouring pads and scrubbers on your acrylic or fiberglass-finished tubs or shower walls.

♦ However, if the finish is already scratched up or marked, you can sometimes remove many of the scratches and marks with a little metal polish on a cloth.

♦ A good way to clean your acrylic baths and shower walls is to rub with a solution of 1 tablespoon ammonia, 1 tablespoon white vinegar, 1 teaspoon water softener and ¾ cup warm water.

Enamel Bath Time... For stubborn stains on enamel tubs, often a little mineral spirits or turpentine will remove it. Follow with some hot dish soap. For the yellow rust marks you may need to add a little salt to the turpentine-soaked cloth.

♦ Kerosene also does a good job of cleaning enamel tubs and sinks. Wash off with hot water and dish soap.

♦ If you need a mild abrasive effect, but are afraid of damaging the surface, use a piece of old net or lace curtain to scour with.

Decal Dilemma...
To remove unwanted bath decals, try heating them with a hair dryer and prying them off with a plastic  spatula. Sometimes, if you leave a little petroleum jelly on to soak through, it will help loosen them enough to remove. Make sure you wash the petroleum jelly off thoroughly afterward. We don't want any slipping and sliding!

♦ Other glue solvents that may remove decals are linseed oil, acetone, lighter fluid and waterless hand cleaner.

Bath-Mat Cleaning... Soak the rubber mat for 2 hours in 1 cup water softener and 8 cups warm water. Scour well and rinse off with clean water. Repeat if necessary.

SINKS...

Enamel-Sink Time... A good all-purpose sink cleaner is distilled white vinegar. Wipe it on with a cloth and then rinse off with clean water. Removes soap film, etc.

◆ An easy way to get your enamel or porcelain sink really white is to lay some paper towels in the sink and soak them with bleach. Leave for an hour or so and then rinse well. Do not follow with any cleaners that contain ammonia.

◆ Another good cleaner and stain remover for your enamel or porcelain sink, is a paste of cream of tartar and hydrogen peroxide. Apply it, let it sit for a short while and then rinse off.

Green Marks... If your ceramic sink has developed those pesky greenish marks, try this. Wet a cloth with white vinegar and then dip it into some table salt. Rub the area briskly with the cloth and then rinse it well.

Rust Marks... For really hard-to-remove rust stains on your porcelain sinks, tubs and toilets, try rubbing the area with automotive rubbing compound on a cloth.

◆ We've found that, as a last resort, a pumice stone works wonders on rust and hard watermarks on porcelain. Make sure you buy the right pumice stone for the surface you're using it on.

Faucet Facts... A good way to clean your bathroom taps (or any chrome for that matter) is to rub it with half a lemon dipped into some salt. If you don't have a lemon, just use distilled white vinegar and salt on a cloth. Rinse well in both cases with water and buff dry with a dry cloth or paper towel.

♦ If you're fortunate enough to be able to afford gold-plated bathroom fittings, it's safest to use only a damp cloth.

Hair Remover... Before you start cleaning your tub, sink or shower, make sure you remove all traces of hair first. If the area is dry, use a vacuum; if wet, use a damp cloth. It'll make your job a lot easier.

Plug Pitting... If you're using a bathroom cleanser on your sink or tub, make sure you rinse the metal area around the drain plug well, otherwise it could cause corrosion and pitting of the metal.

(Spa)rkling... Here's a good way to keep hard-water deposits off your whirlpool-tub surfaces. Pour in 3 or 4 tablespoons dish-washer detergent and turn on the pump for a few minutes. Then drain.

Pop Plumbing... Sounds crazy, but in an emergency you can often unplug a sink, bathtub or shower drain by pouring 2 or 3 cans of cola down the drain hole. Leave for an hour or so.

SHOWER SHAKE-UPS

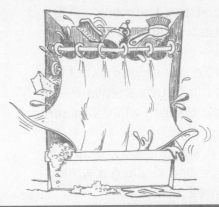

SHOWER DOORS AND CURTAINS...

Shower Doors... Wash the doors with distilled white vinegar. It's wonderful for removing soap scum and buildup.

♦ If that leftover bottle of white wine has gone sour on you, use it on your shower door instead of throwing it out. Rinse off with water and dry well...even if it's a dry wine!

♦ Or you can wipe the shower door down with some fabric softener on a damp cloth. Buff with a clean, dry cloth.

♦ To prevent that unsightly soap scum from returning as quickly, wipe your shower doors down with some lemon oil. You should find you won't have to clean them as often.

♦ If you don't have any lemon oil, often a little baby oil will work as well.

♦ Furniture polish buffed on the door can also do the trick.

Shower-Door Runners... A good scrub with some white tooth- paste on an old toothbrush should clean out most of the buildup. Brush afterward with some distilled white vinegar.

♦ A stiff-bristled paintbrush dipped in vinegar works well too.

Door-Runner Maintenance... After you shower, run the sponge head of a small sponge paintbrush along the bottom runner channels. It's ideal for keeping them dry and as a result, mildew free.

Shower Curtains... Soap film is quickly and easily removed from plastic shower curtains. Place several large bath towels in the washing machine along with the shower curtain. Add ½ cup vinegar. Remember to remove the curtain before the spin cycle starts and hang it up immediately.

♦ If the curtain has very bad mildew on it, clean as above, but **replace** the ½ cup vinegar with ½ cup chlorine bleach.

♦ Prevent soap film buildup on the bottom of your plastic shower curtains by rubbing baby oil on the area.

Curtain Up... It makes sense that if you keep your shower curtain closed it'll be less likely to develop mildew deposits.

Curtain Down... Many people are starting to use just the fabric outer curtain and removing the plastic inner curtain. It saves cleaning the plastic curtain, and if you tuck the fabric curtain into the tub when showering, it is usually waterproof enough to keep your floor dry. Don't forget to wring it as dry as you can when leaving the tub and close it to it's full width. This will help prevent mildew gathering in the folds.

SHOWER WALLS, GROUT AND SUCH...

Shower Walls... Try cleaning the walls and the tiled floor of your shower with ordinary dishwasher detergent. Apply the detergent; let it sit for 2 or 3 hours and then scrub. Use a sponge mop to reach high areas and also to save you bending down to do the floor. Your back will thank you for it!

♦ It's a good idea to always rub the walls and door down with a squeegee before you get out of the shower. This will help prevent those water spots. If you don't have a squeegee, use an old window-wiper blade.

Tiled And Acrylic Shower Walls...

To remove those moldy spots on your shower walls, wash with a solution of 1 teaspoon water softener and ¾ cup warm water, 1 tablespoon ammonia and 1 tablespoon vinegar. Wash well followed by a clean water rinse. Buff dry.

♦ For tile maintenance: once you've cleaned your tiled shower walls, wipe lemon oil or furniture polish, or even car wax, on the tiles. It helps keep the soap film from sticking to the walls.

Showerhead Cleaning... To remove hard-water deposits and keep your showerhead flowing freely, fill a container with half hot water and half vinegar. Let soak for an hour or two.

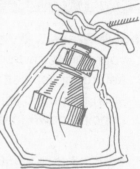

♦ If you don't want to remove the showerhead, pour 2 or 3 inches of vinegar into a small plastic sandwich bag and place it over the whole head. Tape it in place and leave overnight.

Grout Grime... Mildew and grime taking over your tile grout? Remove it with a paste of baking soda and ordinary household bleach. Smear the paste onto the grout with a kitchen spatula or similar object. Leave to dry for an hour or two, then scrub it off with a toothbrush and clean water. Do not follow with any cleaner that has ammonia as an ingredient. Works well on rust stains too!

♦ A paste of borax and lemon juice will often remove grime and mold from tile grout. Let it dry before scrubbing it off with an old toothbrush for the full effect.

♦ Ammonia will usually deal with really stubborn mildew deposits on your grout. Put rubber gloves on and apply with an old toothbrush. Do NOT follow with bleach.

♦ A really extreme, but effective, grout cleaner is oven cleaner. Spray it on a small section and wipe it off within 2 to 3 seconds and rinse with water IMMEDIATELY. Then move on to the next section. You should wear rubber gloves and leave the shower area open and well ventilated.

♦ For caulking between the wall and the tub, leave a rolled cloth soaked with bleach on it for 3 to 4 hours. Rinse well with clean water. Do not follow with a cleaner with ammonia as an ingredient.

 **Please Your Plants...** In the summer, when you decide to take a cool shower, give your houseplants a cleaning at the same time by bringing them into the shower with you. They'll respond well to the humidity and moisture, and who knows, you might respond well to the "tropical" environment!

Double Duty... Why not clean the shower when you next take one. It'll save you having to make the time to do it... and think about it, you certainly won't get your clothes wet like last time!

TOILET TREATMENT

EVERYTHING TO DO WITH TOILETS...

Toilet-Ring Tricks... Remove stubborn toilet rings with a paste of lemon juice and borax. Allow to set before scrubbing.

♦ You might also try this method. Pour a cup or two of white vinegar into the toilet bowl, let it sit overnight, then brush well and flush.

♦ A good maintenance cleaner for your toilet bowl is ordinary baking soda. It also helps with those toilet odors.

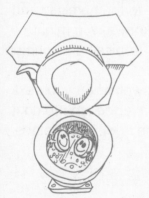

♦ Another environment-friendly toilet cleaner is the seldom-used denture tablet. Depending on how bad the stain is, simply drop 2 or 3 tablets in the bowl water. Let stand for 2 to 3 hours and brush well and flush.

♦ Another solution you might want to try is pouring a can of cola into the bowl. Leave to sit overnight if possible. Brush well the next day.

Toilet Rust Stains... Many rust stains on your
toilet bowl can be cleaned off with a paste
of cream of tartar and hydrogen peroxide.

♦ Fine sandpaper or a pumice stone will
usually remove really bad rust stains.

Toilet-Rim Tip... Make sure you put your cleaner on a
stiff-bristled toilet brush and get it right under the rim.
Otherwise the holes there that release the water will
tend to clog up.

Toilet Warning... I don't
believe in cleaning a toilet
with bleach. If you forget
and use a cleaner that has
ammonia in it, as soon as
the ammonia mixes with any
bleach residue, you could
get very toxic fumes. Think about it: urine has some
ammonia in it too. I'm staying away from bleach in my toilet!

Toilet-Tank Tip... A clever way to keep those hard-water
deposits from forming in your tank is to drop in a denture
tablet once every 6 weeks or so. Leave overnight, brush
and flush.

Toilet-Level Tip... Take a bucketful of water and throw the
contents into the toilet bowl before you start cleaning it.
This actually forces the water level down in the toilet bowl
and allows you to access those bowl rings, etc., easier.

Toilet-Plunger Tip... It's a good idea to rub some ordinary automotive grease or petroleum jelly around the rim of your rubber toilet plunger. This helps provide a good seal for your plunger when it comes time to unclog your toilet.

Toilet-Brush Off... Keep all those ugly bacteria off your toilet brush by swishing it around in a 50/50 solution of bleach and water every couple of weeks or so. Don't forget to rinse it off thoroughly with soap and water afterward and don't clean it with a cleaner that contains ammonia.

♦ We prefer to use the brushes that have a plastic bristle core rather than a metal wire core. The plastic is less likely to mark the surface of your toilet bowl.

Vacation Tip... It's usually not a good idea to leave any toilet cleaner in the toilet bowl while you're away from home... even for a weekend. The cleaner sitting in the water may harm the surface of the toilet bowl if it is left on too long.

♦ What you can do, though, is stretch a sheet of plastic cling wrap over the bowl and leave it on while you're away from home. This will help stop the water evaporating too quickly and will keep the water level constant, which, in turn, helps keep the toilet rings away.

IN GENERAL

WALLS, FLOORS AND CEILINGS...

Tiled Walls... A good cleaning recipe for tiled bathroom walls is 1 cup ammonia, 1 cup vinegar and ½ cup water softener in a bucket of warm water. Rinse well. Do NOT follow with a bleach cleaner.

♦ If you have guests arriving and you just don't have time to clean those offensive mold spots off the tile grout, I'm not above rubbing a little white shoe polish on them. You can always clean it off after they leave, can't you?

♦ What if you don't have any of that white shoe polish? Well, you can always use white office correction liquid!

Steam Cleaning... If you open the hot-water faucet in your shower a few minutes before attacking the grime in your bathroom, the steam build-up will help make the cleanup that much easier.

Vacuum First... Before taking on the task of washing your bathroom floor, vacuum up all the dust and hair first. It'll make your cleanup task a lot easier and a lot less messy.

Tiled Floors... A good tiled-floor cleaner for your bathroom floor is 1 cup ammonia, 1 cup distilled white vinegar and ½ cup water softener in a bucket of warm water. Rinse well. Do NOT follow with bleach or a cleaner containing bleach.

Minty-Fresh Floors... A great cleaner, deodorizer and bacteria destroyer for tiled bathroom floors is, believe it or not, mouthwash! Just mix about half a cup of it in about two quarts of hot water.

Moldy Ceiling... To remove those mold spots on your bathroom ceiling, wash with a mop soaked in a solution of one part water softener and 6 parts water. Rinse and dry well.

♦ Another method is to use a solution of ¼ cup bleach to 1 gallon water. I'd suggest you wear eye and clothing protection with this method. Rinse well and dry. Do not follow with a cleaner that contains ammonia as an ingredient.

♦ Remember that oil repels moisture, which in turn can cause mold. So it follows that you may want wipe your ceilings every so often with a little baby oil on a cloth. Use a covered sponge mop to make it easier.

OTHER BATHROOM TRICKS...

Save Time... Take advantage of the time when you're watching over your children in the bathtub. Clean up areas of the bathroom while they're playing with their rubber duckies!

Medicine-Cabinet Care... If your cabinet has a toothbrush rack, make sure you keep it clean. Rub down often with a cloth dampened with distilled white vinegar, which is both a cleaner and a mild disinfectant. Sometimes a cotton-tipped swab dampened with vinegar is great for cleaning out all the little areas.

Mirror Mess... If you use hair spray, you'll find that it often leaves a film on the surface of your bathroom mirror. The best way to clean this off is by wiping it down with rubbing alcohol.

Soap Sponge... Stick a sharp knife in the end of a thick sponge (preferably cellulose) and slit open a small compartment down the center of the sponge. Now you can slip all those small leftover soap slivers into the "pocket" and you have a wonderful automatic-sudsing sponge.

Damp Odor... One way to help cut down on moisture and that damp smell in your bathroom is to place several chunks of charcoal in a margarine tub and leave it in one or two of the cupboards. Replace the charcoal every 3 months or so.

Homemade Disinfectant... An all-round disinfectant recipe is 1 tablespoon bleach to 1 gallon hot water. NOT to be used in toilets, or followed with a cleaner that contains ammonia as an ingredient.

~ ♦ ~

CHAPTER 4

FOILING FURNITURE FOES

HOW NOT TO TAKE GRIME SITTING DOWN!

GOING WITH THE GRAIN

POLISHING AND DUSTING...

Furniture Filosophy... Much of the furniture in your home came from the factory with a finish that protects it from day-to-day wear and tear. The reason to use waxes, polishes and cleaners on your furniture, however, is two-fold. First, you want to remove deposits like smoke, grease, dust, etc.; and second, you want it to bring out the item's luster.

Homemade Furniture Polishers... A great homemade polish can be made from ⅓ cup of white vinegar, ⅓ cup of turpentine and ⅓ cup of boiled linseed oil. Add 4 teaspoons almond extract for a pleasant fragrance. Bottle it and shake well before using. Apply with a soft damp cloth and polish with another clean lint-free cloth.

♦ Another polish recipe is a mixture of 3 parts olive oil and 1 part lemon oil.

♦ If you don't have lemon oil, use 1 teaspoon olive oil and 1 cup white vinegar.

♦ Remember that you can often replace lemon oil with mineral oil, because that is what many lemon oils have as a base.

Polish Smarts... When choosing a polish or wood treatment, you may want to avoid ingredients like alcohol and ammonia.

♦ An old trick is to apply your polish with a cloth dampened with a little water. You'll find the polish will go on a lot easier.

♦ Remember that "boiled" linseed oil doesn't mean you have to boil it first. You definitely don't want to do that. You can buy boiled linseed oil direct from your store. It dries fairly quickly, unlike raw linseed oil, which virtually never dries. Because of this, it's something you don't usually want to use on your furniture.

Waxing... A good hard car wax can often be used on furniture. Some people prefer it to oil-based polishes that can attract dust.

Emergency Waxing... Company coming and no time to wax your furniture? You can usually get a pretty nice shine by simply rubbing with a fresh sheet of wax paper. Buff afterward with a soft cloth.

Dusting Awkward Areas... Use an ordinary hair dryer, or, for those really hard-to-reach spots, a small bicycle pump!

♦ For hard-to-reach areas, spray the
bristles of a paintbrush with
your homemade furniture
polish to dust and polish at
the same time.

Dust-Cloth Treatment... To make
your dust cloths more efficient, mix
a solution of 1 cup warm water, 1 tablespoon boiled
linseed oil, ½ teaspoon dish soap and ½ teaspoon
ammonia. Soak the dust cloth in the mixture and let it
dry. It's best to store them in sealed containers.

CLEANING AND STAIN REMOVAL...

Black Lacquer Furniture... Grate some mild hand soap
into a bowl of warm water. Dampen a soft cloth with the
solution and wipe away those smudges and fingerprints
easily. Dry the surfaces immediately with a soft, dry
buffing cloth.

Glass-Top Furniture... For pieces like coffee tables and
tea trolleys that have glass tops, the glass can be
cleaned with ordinary distilled white vinegar on a soft,
lint-free cloth.

♦ If the base to your glass top is chrome, clean the
chrome parts with apple cider vinegar or rubbing
alcohol.

Cleaning Off The Polish... To remove dirty oil and wax buildup from your wooden furniture, try cleaning the surface of
the piece with a soft cloth dipped in mineral spirits.

Prevention Is Better Than Cure... Where possible, use coasters. But choose them wisely. If you can find wooden ones that have a liner that is absorbent and a layer of felt on the base, they should serve you best. And if they have a raised edge to contain any small leak or spill, so much the better.

♦ You can devise your own table pad to protect your table from hot containers and spills by going to an upholsterer. Ask them to cut a piece of lined upholstery vinyl to the size of your tabletop. This way you can match the color of the pad to either the table or your décor. A lace throw should finish the look nicely.

♦ To safeguard against water-marks on your dining table at your next dinner party, wrap plastic cling wrap over the top surface and place your tablecloth over it.

Water Rings... To remove water rings from wooden furniture, apply regular mayonnaise liberally over them and leave at least 3 to 4 hours, preferably overnight. Wipe off with a soft cloth the next day and that usually does the trick.

Water Spots... Mix ½ teaspoon lemon oil and 1 cup denatured alcohol. Wipe the mixture on the area and buff it dry immediately.

Candle Wax From Wood... To remove candle-wax spills from wooden furniture, soften the wax first with your hair dryer  set on a medium heat. When it starts to melt the wax, wipe the wax off with a soft cloth or paper towel immediately and continue heating the area. Once all the wax deposit is removed, wipe the area with a mild distilled white vinegar and water solution and polish the surface as usual.

♦ Another way to remove excess wax is to hold an ice cube on it for as long as it takes to harden it (usually 3 to 5 minutes). This makes the wax brittle and you should be able to carefully pry it off the surface with a wooden spoon or plastic kitchen spatula.

Paint Removal... If the paint has already dried, try applying some raw linseed oil. Let the piece sit until the paint softens up and then scrape it off with a plastic or wooden utensil.

General Stain Removal... Some good all-purpose stain removers for wooden furniture are lemon extract, oil of peppermint and of course, as a last resort, white toothpaste.

♦ Remember: when removing stains and marks, always start with the gentlest method first. Repeat this method several times before trying a more drastic solution.

REMOVING MARKS AND SCRATCHES...

Treating Heat Marks... Remove heat marks from varnished or shellacked wood surfaces by dabbing spirits of camphor on the spot with a soft cloth. Allow to dry, then polish.

Label Removal... Most paper and porous labels can be removed by rubbing them with baby oil. Let the oil soak through well and scrape carefully with a plastic spatula or wooden spoon.

♦ Or soak the label with your homemade furniture polish.

Burns On Wooden Furniture... Mix vegetable oil with powdered pumice or rottenstone to make a paste. Apply it to the burned area only, rubbing it gently into the grain. Wipe the area clean and polish the piece as usual.

♦ Some burn marks can be removed by rubbing briskly with a paste of cold water and cigarette ash. You can also try substituting cooking oil for the water.

♦ Or try rubbing the area lightly with nail-polish remover.

♦ Boiled linseed oil or petroleum jelly often works as well.

♦ You can also camouflage the mark by blending different colored markers to match the color of the surrounding surface.

♦ Whatever method you use, once the mark is gone you can usually fill the indent by applying several coats of clear nail polish. Allow the nail polish to dry between coats.

Scratches... If your furniture develops small scratches, you can often mask the damage pretty well with a little shoe polish. Blend different colors, if necessary, to match the color of the wood.

♦ Shoe polish makes a pretty nifty emergency furniture polish as well!

♦ Children's wax crayons also work really well because there is a larger variety of colors to blend together. In a pinch, felt-tip markers may do the trick as well.

♦ Pencil crayons also blend well to fill in and disguise scratches.

♦ For light scratches on unlaquered furniture, you can often use the mild rubbing compound used on automobile finishes. Just rub on and off with a damp rag. If the surface finish is left a little dull afterward, that can usually be shined up with some hard car or floor wax.

Chew Marks... Keep your dog (and any other wood-chewing animal you might own) from gnawing at your furniture by wiping down the accessible areas with oil of cloves.

Location, Location, Location... Try to keep your wooden furniture out of any direct sunlight for any prolonged periods. It has a drying-out effect on the furniture surface.

Chair Coasters... Attach corn plasters to the bottom of your chair legs. They'll help prevent marks and scratches on your floor.

CLEANING UP(HOLSTERY)

NB: When using any uphol-stery treatments we always recommend you test an inconspicuous area first for colorfastness.

Read The Label... Always check what the label on the item recommends. Some fabrics allow cleaning with water, some with water and solvents and others suggest only vacuuming.

CLEANING...

Upholstery Shampoo... Use ½ cup powdered or liquid detergent, 1 teaspoon ammonia, 1 teaspoon vinegar and 1 quart of warm water. Mix in a bowl with a hand mixer to work up a good froth. Using the froth only, rub lightly with sponge or cloth over the entire panel or area. Wipe off with a damp cloth or sponge, or use a wet/dry vacuum. Stay off the piece until it is completely dry.

Vinyl-Upholstery Cleaner... Baking soda applied with a damp cloth or sponge will clean and deodorize at the same time.

Canvas-Upholstery Cleaner... For those modern sling-type canvas chairs, washing them with a warm solution of soapy water usually does the trick. Let it air-dry well before sitting in it.

♦ To clean off minor marks from canvas-covered items, without having to wash them, try rubbing them with a clean pencil eraser.

Vacuum First... You'll find it'll make your shampooing job a lot easier if you remove the dust first by vacuuming the upholstery.

And Vacuum Last... If you discover when shampooing your upholstery that it has got a little more wet than you needed it to, simply vacuum the excess moisture out with a wet/dry vacuum attachment.

Pet Hair... Pet hair is easy to remove from uphol-stery. Just rub it off with a rubber dishwashing glove. You'll find the fingers are great for accessing awkward areas.

♦ Some people use a fabric-softener sheet the same way.

♦ Or you can even use a cloth, dampened with a little water.

Nonshrink Slipcovers... If you
have washed your slipcovers,
place them back on the furniture while they're still a little
damp. This way they're more
likely to dry to the right shape.

♦ If they need a little ironing,
simply iron them while
they're on the furniture. Just make sure to use a
warm or cool iron if the cushions happen to have
foam inside.

Nonslip Slipcovers... A great way to stop slipcovers
from moving around is to use a heavy curtain rod as a
weight to hold down the cover. Tuck it under or behind
the cushions, out of sight.

STAIN REMOVAL...

General Stain Remover... Mix about 2 teaspoons dish detergent with ½ cup cool water and whisk until frothy. Apply
the suds by dabbing with a sponge, then remove any
residue soap with a damp cloth.

♦ Club soda can often be dabbed onto a spill to prevent
it setting.

♦ Many greasy stains can often be removed by making
a thick paste of ordinary talcum powder and cold
water. Apply the paste, let it dry and then vacuum the
residue off.

Pet "Accidents"... For dog or cat urine, immediately mix a solution of 2 teaspoons dish soap and cool water. Froth it up and blot the area well with the foamy lather. Wash off with a mixture of white vinegar and water (1 part vinegar to 8 parts water). Make sure you dry the area immediately with a hair dryer set on cool or even a small fan.

Wine Stains... For red- or white-wine spills, sponge immediately with club soda.

♦ Or sprinkle salt over the area immediately to absorb the wine.

♦ For stubborn red-wine stains, mix equal parts of borax and baking soda with a little water to form a paste. Apply the paste to the spill and then wipe it off with a damp cloth. Let it dry. Check for colorfastness first with this method.

Ketchup And Tomato-Based Stains... Using a sponge or absorbent cloth, dab the area with

a mixture of 1 teaspoon mild detergent and 1 cup of cool water. Then follow by dabbing with a solution of 2 teaspoons ammonia and ½ cup water (test for colorfastness first). Apply the detergent solution again and sponge off with clean, cool water. Blot dry.

Other Stains... See the "Specks, Spots And Spills" section in the Wash-Day Wisdom chapter. Many of the clothing stain-removal tips in this chapter can apply to upholstery. Be careful of overwetting though and check first for colorfastness.

Sofa Sunstroke... Make sure you keep your furniture away from direct sunlight. It can fade most fabrics quicker than you'd imagine.

LEATHER LUSTER

CLEANING AND TREATING...

Type Testing... To determine whether you have the kind of leather that can stain permanently (dyed leather), or not (pigmented leather), try the water drop test. Let a drop of water fall on an inconspicuous part of the leather. If it soaks in immediately, then so will the stains. If it doesn't soak in, then you'll know you at least have a chance of removing certain stains.

Pigmented Leather Furniture... In general, leather shouldn't be wet too much. Most water-based stains like cola, red wine, mustard, etc. can often be removed with a damp cloth.

♦ If that method doesn't work, try a cloth dampened with the foamy lather from a very mild soap flake and water solution. Always check for colorfastness first though.

♦ Moderate ink stains can sometimes be removed from certain leather by rubbing the area with baking soda. Wipe off with a damp cloth. Check for color-fastness first.

♦ A good all-purpose cleaner for leather is saddle soap. Using a cloth dampened with water, rub the lather only into the leather. Once dry, buff with a soft cloth.

♦ If you want a leather condi-tioner, try mixing 1 cup boiled linseed oil and ½ cup distilled white vinegar. Shake the mixture well and apply sparingly with a damp cloth. Let dry and buff with a soft cloth.

♦ **Remember** to always test an inconspicuous area of the item before applying anything to your furniture.

♦ Believe it or not, mildew can sometimes be removed from leather by applying a little antiseptic mouthwash to the area with a soft cloth.

Dyed Leather... Don't take a chance. Call in the professionals!

Suede Leather... If you insist on taking the chance, certain marks can sometimes be removed from suede by applying steam with a clothes steamer and a very light rubbing with an emery board. Personally, I'd call in the professionals.

Heat-Sensitive Sofas... It's a good idea to keep your leather furniture away from heat sources, like radiators, heat registers and direct sunlight. Leather could crack under those conditions.

WICKER AND CANE CARE

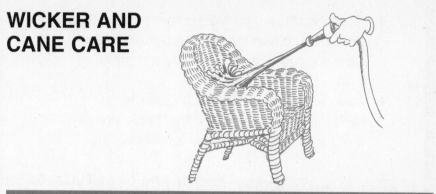

CLEANING AND CONDITIONING...

Wicker Cleaning... Clean wicker furniture by rubbing with a stiff brush dipped in warm salt water. The salt should prevent the wicker from yellowing. Be careful not to wet the wicker too much.

♦ For really stubborn dirt, you may have to take a chance and wet it a bit more. Try cleaning with a solution of 1 part water softener to 8 parts water. Wipe off with a clean wet cloth and let dry. Do not use heat to dry the piece, or you run the risk of the wicker cracking.

♦ Most of the time a good vacuuming is all that wicker needs.

♦ If you prefer, you can plug your hose into the exhaust port and blow the dust off. If your vacuum cleaner does not allow this option, use a hair dryer set on cool.

Cane Cleaning... To clean cane, add a little lemon juice and salt to some warm water. Using a stiff brush, scrub the cane well with the solution. This method should also help prevent the cane from yellowing.

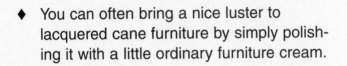

◆ Some warm soapy water mixed with a little borax can clean marks and dirt deposits off cane pretty well. Let it dry naturally.

◆ You can often bring a nice luster to lacquered cane furniture by simply polishing it with a little ordinary furniture cream.

Wicker And Cane TLC... Because of their origins, most wicker and cane furniture pieces enjoy a humid environment. So you may want to get a humidifier if you don't already have one.

◆ Sometimes you can restore dried wicker with a little lemon oil.

◆ Wicker doesn't like really cold temperatures, so make sure you bring your wicker furniture inside during the winter months.

PRIME-
PIECE
PAMPERING

FURNITURE...

Wood-Antique Cleaning... Often the best cleaning treatment for wood antiques is a little warm water on a very soft cloth.

♦ To remove the sticky residue from the price tag on the piece you just bought, try this. Dampen a cloth with white vinegar and rub it softly. With a little patience and care, it should come off safely.

♦ To remove the musty odor from antique cupboards, try rubbing the inside of the cupboard with oil of wintergreen.

Wood Antique TLC... Many furniture experts say it's usually not a good idea to use silicone polishes on antique surfaces.

♦ When waxing, don't forget to wax the insides of cupboards, drawers and the underside of chairs and tables.

♦ You may want to wax (nonsilicone wax) your pieces when the weather gets cold and it's time to turn on your heat. You can wax the pieces again when the weather gets warm and it's time to turn the heat off.

♦ Teak furniture may need a little oiling with some tung oil every so often.

♦ Make sure you keep your antiques out of direct sunlight. You may enjoy a suntan, but they certainly don't!

The Dirt On Dusting... It's a good idea to use old flannel sheets and pajamas for dusting antiques. They will be less likely to scratch the surface, and the older the flannel, the less lint.

♦ A feather duster with a plastic core is also a good dusting tool to use.

♦ The new "feather" dusters you can get, with the synthetic dust-attracting fiber material, are my favorite to use.

♦ A genuine chamois does a good job too. The natural oils in the chamois can be enough to actually polish your antiques as well as dusting.

♦ Another method is to simply vacuum the dust off. For wood furniture, make sure you cover the end of the vacuum wand with a soft, thin sock to prevent scratching.

Marquetry Maintenance... The last thing a piece with marquetry on it needs is being wet. Remember to dust only!

Upholstery Maintenance... Sofas and chairs that are upholstered should be vacuumed regularly to keep dust and dirt from damaging the fibers. Use an upholstery attachment on your vacuum wand.

♦ If you need to shampoo old upholstery, make sure you use only the foam from the shampoo and rub it on with a sponge. Clean a complete cushion or panel at a time to prevent moisture lines. Wipe down with a cloth dampened with a little water and immediately vacuum with a wet/dry vacuum with an upholstery attachment. Let the item air-dry.

MISCELLANEOUS...

Kerosene Lamps... To clean and brighten old kerosene lamps, polish them with a little salt on a damp cloth.

Paintings... Clean the surface of your paintings of any dust by dabbing with a piece of fresh white bread. Stay away from soap or water. If you're hesitant to clean it yourself, have it professionally cleaned.

♦ Never use water on picture glass. Moisture could get in behind and destroy the painting. Pour a little white vinegar on a soft cloth and wipe down carefully.

China... Delicate china should be dusted very carefully. An eyebrow brush is ideal.

Coins... Experts say not to polish coins. If you must clean them, use hot water and a soft cloth.

Fabric Restorer... If you have an old patterned fabric that has accidentally been lightened by stain removal, try this. Make a pot of very strong tea, let it cool and dip a cotton ball into it. Carefully dab the faded area with the tea.

Textile Treasures... If washing is necessary, be very careful. Old pieces can sometimes tear from the extra weight once wet.

Old Books... To clean the paged edges, simply wipe with a piece of fresh white bread.

Umbrella Stand... If you're using your antique umbrella stand, line the bottom with a plastic bag. Then cut a thick cellulose sponge to size and place it on top of the plastic. This way, any dripped water will be soaked up by the sponge. Dry out the sponge after every rainfall.

~ ◆ ~

CHAPTER 5

REMOVING THE DIRT UNDERFOOT

SMART IDEAS FOR CARPETS AND FLOORS!

CLEVER CARPET CLEANING

NB: We always recommend you test any carpet treatment on an inconspicuous area first. This will help determine its colorfastness.

CLEANING...

Preshampoo... Before you shampoo, it's a good idea to vacuum your carpet thoroughly. This will make the job much easier and considerably less messy.

Shampoo Planning... Always begin shampooing your carpet at the end farthest from the doorway and work your way toward that doorway. This will prevent you from stepping on the cleaned area before it dries and ruining your shampoo job!

Shampoo Schedule... The general rule of thumb is to shampoo your carpet every year. Of course this is dependant on the traffic it gets. Judge accordingly.

♦ A clever idea for wall-to-wall carpeting is to keep a piece of the carpet when you lay it. When your carpet sample appears a lot lighter than your carpeting, it's time to give it a good shampoo.

Carpet And Rug Shampoo... Use ½ cup powdered or liquid detergent, 1 teaspoon ammonia, 1 teaspoon vinegar and 1 quart of warm water. Mix in a bowl with a hand mixer to work up a good froth. Using the froth only, rub lightly with sponge or cloth over the entire carpet. Allow carpet to dry and vacuum.

♦ Try not to get the carpet too wet when shampooing it, or at the very least, don't leave it that way for too long. Mildew and his pal, odor, are waiting just around the corner!

♦ If you don't have a wet/ dry vacuum you can remove a lot of moisture by rolling the area with a clean paint roller. The thicker and more absorbent the roller, the better.

Carpet Freshener... An easy way to brighten and spruce up that dull carpet is to sprinkle a thin layer of borax over it. Let it sit overnight, then vacuum it well.

♦ Another version is to add twice the amount of corn meal or cornstarch to the borax and treat the carpet as above.

♦ Or add 4 tablespoons regular baby powder and 3 tablespoons corn starch to 1 cup of baking soda and treat the carpet as above.

New-Carpet Odor... To remove that brand-new-carpet smell quickly, crank up the heat in the house to its maximum. Leave the heat on for about 4 or 5 hours. Then turn it off and open the doors and windows to air the room out and cool down the house ... and yourself of course!

New-Carpet Static... To cut down on static from new and nylon-fiber carpets, mix 2 cups fabric softener with 1 gallon of water. Pour into a spray mister and spray the carpet liberally.

Eau De Vacuum... To add a pleasant fragrance to your room and help cut down on musty "vacuum odor" when vacuuming, try this little trick. Moisten a cloth with some fabric softener and secure it with some tape over one-half of the vacuum exhaust port. Be careful not to cover the whole port or your vacuum could overheat and break down.

Clean De Vacuum... Save on vacuum bags. Carefully cut open the top of your full bag and empty the contents out. Fold the top over ½ inch and, using a paper stapler, staple the bag closed at the fold. And if you own a staple remover, you can repeat the procedure as long as the bag lasts.

♦ To remove debris from your stopped-up vacuum hose, simply push a broom or mop handle through it. Be careful not to force it too much or you could damage the hose.

Protect De Vacuum... To prevent small metal objects, like pins and paper clips, being sucked up into your vacuum cleaner, glue several strong, flat magnets to the front underside of the head of the vacuum. The magnets will nab them before they can be picked up by the sweeper bar.

STAIN REMOVAL...

Act Fast!... Most stains are easier to remove if you treat them immediately or as soon as possible. For example, tomato-based stains and pop stains set literally within minutes!

Carpet-Stain Removal...
A good general carpet-stain remover is foamy shaving cream. Simply apply a blob to the area. Rub it in well with a sponge and then rinse the area off with clean water. Let dry overnight and vacuum the next day.

♦ Waterless hand cleaner is great for many different carpet stains like oil, grease and even tomato-based messes.

♦ As far as Turkish, Oriental and Persian rugs are concerned, it's best to have them professionally cleaned.

Blood... For fresh bloodstains, apply foamy shaving cream immediately and rinse off.

♦ For more stubborn bloodstains, make a paste of meat tenderizer and water. Apply it to the stain, let it dry and vacuum.

♦ For really difficult bloodstains, dab the area with a little hydrogen peroxide. Make sure that you rinse it off as soon as possible with cold water.

Burn Mark... For scorched and light burn marks on your carpet, you can often fade the mark considerably by applying a solution of 1 part hydrogen peroxide and 5 parts water.

Candle Wax... Place an ice cube on the wax for 3 to 5 minutes. When brittle, chip off the excess wax with an egg lifter or similar utensil. Then place a folded paper towel over the area and hold a warm- to medium-heat iron on the towel for a few seconds. When you lift the iron you'll see the paper has absorbed the melted wax. Do not move the iron around or you'll spread the wax. Several applications with fresh paper towels are usually necessary.

♦ Any residual die from colored candles can usually be removed by dabbing with a little rubbing alcohol or paint thinner.

Chewing Gum... Hold an ice cube against the chewing gum until it hardens. Then simply lever the gum off with your fingernail.

♦ If there is any residue left on the carpet, it can usually be removed by brushing hard with a toothbrush dipped into some rubbing alcohol or waterless hand cleaner.

Coffee And Tea... Blot as much of the spill with paper towels, then apply distilled white vinegar to the area. If the stain persists, put a blob of foamy shaving cream on the stain, rub it in with a sponge and rinse off with water. Let dry and vacuum.

Fruit Juice... First soak up the excess with paper towels, then sprinkle borax over the area to counteract the acidity in the fruit juice. After an hour or so, rinse with water and let dry.

♦ Really stubborn fruit-juice stains can usually be removed by dabbing them with a little hydrogen peroxide.

Furniture Polish... Blot the area with a little paint thinner. Then immediately rinse off with soapy water and a little white vinegar.

Glue... There's usually one of three things that will remove glue, depending on the type of glue. If you are unsure of the nature of the glue that's on the carpet, try vinegar, soap and water first (general water-based glues). Try acetone second (for most other glues), and paint thinner if the acetone doesn't work.

♦ As a last resort, you may need to snip off any remaining glue left on the surface of your carpet.

Nail Polish... If you've already let it dry, try holding an ice cube on the spill. This should make it more brittle and you may be able to chip off a lot of it. Follow up by dabbing the area with acetone, working from the outside of the spill toward its center. As you dab, blot with a paper towel in order to contain it.

Oil Or Grease Marks... Act fast! Sprinkle about ¼ inch of cornmeal over the area. Rub it in well, let it sit for about an hour, then vacuum.

♦ If the stain persists, rub some waterless hand cleaner (the stuff mechanics
use to get grease off their hands) into
the stain. Rinse off with a little water,
let dry and vacuum.

Pet "Accidents"... Pour liberal amounts of club soda on
the area and blot immediately with paper towels. If the
odor is still there the next day, cover the area with about
¼ inch of baking soda and let it sit on the carpet for
2 days, then vacuum.

♦ If stain or odor still persists, try this method. Add 1 cup
of hydrogen peroxide to 1 tablespoon of baking soda.
Add 1 teaspoon of dish soap and stir well. Apply the
solution to the area with a sponge. Let it dry and
vacuum. Make sure you throw the solution away after
use. Because of its volatility it loses its effectiveness
within a short time.

♦ We've also had some success with a paste of borax
and water. Apply the paste, wait for it to dry and then
give it a good vacuum.

Pop... Soak up excess and then wipe with equal parts white
vinegar and water.

♦ If the stain persists, rub it gently with waterless hand
cleaner and rinse off with a little water.

Red Wine... Club soda should be applied to a red wine stain as soon as possible. However a stubborn (or dried) red wine stain can often be removed by dabbing with a little hydrogen peroxide or a paste of cream of tartar and water.

♦ A paste of equal parts borax and baking powder mixed with cold water is a good red-wine stain remover too.

Rust Marks... Sometimes rust marks can be removed from your carpet by mixing some water with a little baking soda to form a paste. Apply to the stain, let it sit for 3 or 4 hours, then shampoo.

Soot... Scoop up excess soot, then sprinkle talcum powder liberally over the area. Leave for a few minutes and vacuum well.

♦ Or, apply the "Homemade Carpet And Rug Shampoo" recipe.

Tar... Most tar stains can be removed by dabbing the area with a little kerosene on a sponge. Rinse off with warm water with a little dish soap in it.

Tomato-Based Stains... Ketchup, spaghetti sauce, tomato juice, etc. can usually be removed by applying foamy shaving cream and rubbing it in with a sponge. Rinse off and vacuum when dry.

Vomit... Scrape up the excess with a spatula and dust-pan. Apply a solution of ¼ cup baking soda and 1 cup warm water.

♦ To remove the odor, apply the "Pet Accidents" recipe (the one with hydrogen peroxide, baking soda and dish soap).

WOOD FLOORS MADE EASY

POLISHING AND VACUUMING...

Floor Polisher... Make your own floor polish. Add 1 table-spoon beeswax to 2 cups of mineral oil. Get the mixture to melt and blend, by heating it in a double boiler. Allow it to cool and apply to your floor with a soft cloth.

♦ Some cleaning experts say you should polish wooden floorboards with the grain, not across it.

Wax Whoops!... If your wooden floor has a hard sealed finish to it, it is best not to apply wax to it. It could become extremely slippery!

Quick Shine... To bring a quick and easy sparkle to your waxed wooden floors, without a full wax job, take a piece of wax paper and rub it over your floor with a broom or a mop.

Dry And Shine... If you have just cleaned your wooden floor with a liquid floor cleaner, make sure you let it dry completely before applying any floor wax or polish.

Otherwise you may end up with an unattractive, dull grayish finish...and then you'll need another Haley's Hint to remove that!

Floor Fact... Dust and dirt particles can do some pretty bad damage to floors in the form of pitting and scratching. Sweep or vacuum regularly.

Vacuum First... Right before washing or polishing floors, vacuum, or at least sweep the area well first. The washing process will be that much easier.

♦ I prefer to use a canister vacuum with a wand on wooden floors, rather than the kind with a beater bar. If the wand attachment doesn't have a brush edge, place a thin sock or panty hose leg over the end to help prevent scratching the floor.

Floor Heat Registers... Vacuuming regularly is necessary. Every so often you can also remove them and give them a scrub with soapy water. Make sure they're dried well before replacing them.

CLEANING, STAIN REMOVAL AND MAINTENANCE...

Floor Scourer... Try not to use any harsh scourers or steel wool on your wooden floors. Most regular build ups can be removed by rubbing with an ordinary plastic mesh onion bag and a little cleaner.

Floor Cleaner... A good-all round wooden floor cleaner recipe is 4 tablespoons distilled white vinegar, 4 tablespoons water softener and 1 gallon pail of warm water. Wipe dry as you wash.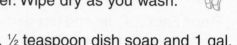

◆ Or mix ¼ cup borax, ½ teaspoon dish soap and 1 gal. warm water.

◆ Another quick floor-cleaner recipe is equal parts distilled white vinegar and warm water. Add a few drops of regular baby oil to add to the shine and the aroma.

Wax Buildup... A good way to remove excess wax from wooden floors, is with a solution of ¼ cup water softener and 4 cups warm water.

◆ To tell if you've removed all the wax from your floor, simply scratch the surface with your fingernail. If you end up with a waxy residue under your nail, keep cleaning!

General Stains... You'd be surprised at how many spills and stains can be removed from wood floors with a little dish soap. Always try it first.

Pet Accidents... To remove the pungent smell of pet urine from your wooden floors, try this method. Mix ½ cup of distilled white vinegar with 2 cups of warm water and wet the area well. Sprinkle some baking soda onto the area and give it a good scrub. As soon as the effervescing stops, rinse well with warm water and dry the floor immediately.

General Scratches... Small scratches can often be disguised by rubbing carefully with a fine steel wool dipped in floor wax.

VINYL, LINOLEUM AND TILE TIPS

A Clean Sweep...
Make sure you sweep the floor well before washing. Crumbs and dust bunnies mixed with your cleaner can make your washing task a lot harder and messier.

LINOLEUM AND CERAMIC FLOORING...

Washing Linoleum Floors... You don't want to get linoleum too wet. Just mop it with a little water and mild detergent. Rinse off with clean water on your mop.

♦ If your linoleum floor is rather old, you may want to try sprucing it up with a wipe down! Just mix equal parts milk and turpentine and buff the linoleum with a soft cloth.

Waxing Linoleum Floors... If you want to have a shiny finish on your old linoleum floor, then you are probably going to have to wax it. Try buffing with a hard floor or automobile wax.

Two Pails Are Better Than One... When washing your solid linoleum or vinyl floors, remember to use two pails. One with the cleaning solution and the other with clean water. Apply the solution to the whole floor and let it sit for 5 minutes or so. Then, using the solution, wash a small area and rinse the cloth or mop in the clean water before washing the next area. This way your cleaning solution remains clean and does a much better job of cleaning your floor.

Make One Your Garbage Pail... Assign your plastic garbage bin as your second wash pail (or both wash pails, if you have more than one). This way you won't have to buy another pail and you get your garbage bin cleaned at the same time!

Ceramic-Tile Cleaning... Wash your glazed ceramic tiles with warm water and just a few drops of dish soap.

♦ It's a good idea to buff the ceramic-tile floor dry immediately to prevent streaking.

♦ A half lemon rubbed on glazed tiles is a good pepper-upper. Buff well.

Grimy Grout... Most stained grout between ceramic floor tiles can be cleaned with a solution of 1 part chlorine bleach and 20 parts water. Apply with a toothbrush. It may be necessary to let the bleach solution sit on the grout for 10 or 15 minutes. Don't follow with a cleaner that has ammonia as an ingredient. Bleach and ammonia should never go together.

VINYL ...

Scratches... Repair minor scratches and indentations by filling with clear nail polish. Apply by using several thin coats and letting each coat dry before applying the next one.

Washing Vinyl Floors... Most popular nowadays is no-wax vinyl flooring. It has a finish that can usually be cleaned with a little liquid detergent or dish soap and water. Rinse with clean water.

♦ When washing self-adhesive floor tiles, use as little water as possible. This will help prevent moisture getting in between the seams which can eventually cause the tile to curl.

To Wax Or Not To Wax... No-wax vinyl flooring doesn't need to be waxed. Hence its name. In fact, if you do wax it, it can cause yellowing.

♦ For waxable vinyl flooring, try to stay away from solvent-based waxes and polishes.

When To Wax... Waxable vinyl flooring should be waxed usually once a month or so. But it's important to make sure you remove the old wax first. To do this best, we like to use a solution of ¼ cup water softener and 4 cups warm water.

How To Wax... First, make quite sure the floor is completely dry, then apply a light coat of wax. Let the floor dry for about half an hour and then apply a second light coat of wax.

Stains... Most scuff marks and many stains can be easily removed from tile with a pencil eraser or some toothpaste on a cloth.

♦ We've also had great success with ordinary cheap hair spray!

THE REST OF THE FLOORS

GENERAL FLOOR CLEANING...

Brick Floors... Clean your brick floors by washing them with warm water and a mild powdered detergent. Rinse them well.

Concrete Floors... Indoor concrete floors are usually sealed. To clean them, wash with a damp cloth, or mop and a little dish soap.

Cork Floors... It's a good idea not to wet cork flooring too much. It could make it swell and lift.

♦ If the cork floor is sealed, you can usually clean it with a solution of ½ cup distilled white vinegar to 1 pail of water.

♦ If the floor is not sealed, it's usually best to buff it with a hard wax polish 2 or 3 times a year.

Marble Floors... Wash with a little warm water and a few drops of dish soap. Dry immediately.

♦ For stubborn stains, rub with a paste of lemon juice and baking soda.

Quarry Tile Floors... Wipe down every so often with a little mineral oil to restore the luster.

Slate Floors... Wash slate floors with a mixture of ½ teaspoon dish soap and 1 gallon warm water. Rinse off with clean warm water and buff the floor with a little milk if you so choose.

Stone Floors... Always wet the floor before applying any cleaner.

♦ Rinse really well afterward to prevent the surface chipping.

♦ Avoid cleaning with acids. They can cause pitting.

Straw Mats... Mix 1 gallon warm water with ½ cup salt, ½ cup water softener and ¼ cup lemon juice. Sponge mixture on and let air-dry.

~ ♦ ~

CHAPTER 6

WALLS AND WINDOWS

CLEANING UP AND CLEANING DOWN!

WALL AND WOODWORK WONDERS

WALL CLEANING...

Painted-Wall Cleaner... For a good all-round cleaning solution for washable painted walls, mix 1 part of ammonia and 1 part white vinegar to 16 parts of warm water. If you like, you can also add 3 or 4 tablespoons of dish soap or even baking soda. Wipe well and rinse with clean water.

♦ Or wash with a solution of 2 tablespoons water softener and 1 gallon of warm water.

♦ Another method is to use ½ cup borax, mixed with 1 bucket of warm water and 1 teaspoon dish soap.

♦ To prevent your washing solution becoming dirty too quickly, and putting some of the dirt you've taken off right back on, use two pails instead of one. Fill one with the cleaning solution and leave the other one empty. As you wash, wring out the cloth or sponge into the empty pail. This keeps your cleaning solution a clean solution!

Paneled-Wall Cleaner... A little dish soap in a bucket of water will usually clean paneled walls of everyday build-up. Dry off as you wash.

Crayon Removal... A little toothpaste on a dry cloth.

 ♦ You can also try a cloth dampened with some lighter fluid. Be careful though, it's extremely flammable. After all, it is lighter fluid!

 ♦ Baking soda often does the trick too.

Marker Removal... On most wash-able walls you can rub gently with a dry cloth and toothpaste.

 ♦ Hair spray works well for enamel painted walls, but make sure you have a cloth to wipe it off before the dissolved marker runs down the wall.

Nicotine Removal... Of course the best way not to have nicotine stained walls (and lungs) is not to smoke at all. However to clean already stained walls, dip a rag into some distilled white vinegar and wash from the bottom up (that way you don't get streaks from the solution running down the wall). It usually works pretty well, depending on how badly stained the wall is.

 ♦ Sometimes all you need to do is to rub the walls down with some ordinary liquid dish soap and rinse with clean water.

♦ A more extreme method is to wipe the walls down with a cloth dipped in ammonia and then wash off immediately with clean water. Wear gloves and make sure you open all doors and windows to keep the room well ventilated. You may even want to put a strong fan behind you at an angle so as to blow away the harsh fumes from the ammonia.

♦ If the nicotine stain is really bad, you may have to repaint the wall. However, it's a good idea to first remove the tar by washing it down with a solution of TSP (trisodium phosphate), but make sure you follow the directions on the label as it is pretty strong stuff.

Wooden Baseboards And Molding... Remember, before washing your walls, always give the baseboards and top molding a quick going over with the vacuum cleaner wand. Or rub them down with a damp rag. This removes any dust, dirt, etc. that is just waiting to attach itself to your cleaning cloth or sponge as you wash the wall.

Wood Direction... For wood-grain molding it's best to follow the direction of the grain.

WALLPAPER CLEANING...

Fabric-Wall Cleaner... It's usually best to vacuum walls covered in fabric like velvet, burlap, grass cloth, etc.

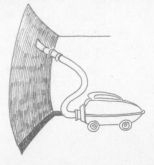

Wallpaper Cleaner... Most wallpaper nowadays is washable. Clean with a little dish soap in a pail of warm water. Not too wet though!

♦ Or mix 2 tablespoons ammonia with 4 cups warm water.

Wallpaper Marks... Many marks can be removed from wallpaper with an Artgum eraser or a dry sponge.

♦ For general grease marks, apply a paste of baking soda (or fuller's earth) and water. Let dry and wipe off with a damp cloth.

♦ For waxy grease marks, like candle wax and wax crayon, hold a folded paper towel over the spot and place a medium-heat iron against the towel. Most of the wax will melt into the paper towel. Residual coloring can usually be removed with a little rubbing alcohol.

♦ Many stains and marks can be treated as you would on painted walls. Test on an inconspicuous area first.

Removing Wallpaper... Remember to always score the surface of the wallpaper first with a fork or sharp knife. This allows the cleaner to penetrate better.

♦ Often wallpaper can be removed by soaking well with warm water and dish soap and then scraping with a wallpaper scraper.

♦ Many people swear by a solution of equal parts white vinegar and hot water. Soak it really well and then keep soaking it until you see the paper really bubbling. Follow up with your scraper.

WINDOWS AND DRESSINGS

WINDOWS...

How To Wash Windows... Always wash your windows with horizontal strokes on the inside and vertical strokes on the outside, or vice versa. This way, if there are any streaks, you'll know which side of the glass they're on!

How To Wash Frigid Windows... If it's really cold, windows can sometimes tend to fog up when you're applying the cleaner directly to the window. Try adding the cleaner to the cleaning rag instead, it might help.

Homemade Window Cleaner... Mix ¼ cup of white vinegar and ¼ cup of ammonia into a bucket half filled with warm water. Fill several spray bottles or plant misters and you'll have an excellent cleaner as well as a long-lasting supply. To give your homemade window cleaner a "professional" appeal, try adding a drop of blue food coloring and a few drops of lemon extract to each container and shake well.

♦ Another good window cleaner is a mixture of ½ cup of cornstarch to 1 gallon of warm water. Rinse with a little white vinegar.

♦ Our neighbor at the cottage brings a shine to her windows by cleaning them in a solution made from onions and water. Simply chop up a medium onion into eighths and drop it into half a bucket of warm water and wash away.

Frost-Free Windows... Add 2 tablespoons of rubbing alcohol to a container of "Homemade Window Cleaner" to help prevent frost forming on the inside of the windows.

♦ Or apply a solution of 1 part salt and 8 parts water to the window.

Hard-Water Spray... Neat white vinegar usually removes most spots caused by the minerals in hard-water spray.

Fly Spots... A little denatured alcohol will usually get rid of those ugly fly spots on windows.

♦ Cold tea works as well.

Paint Spots... A little linseed oil loosens up most dried paint spots on windows.

- ◆ Or soak the paint in equal parts ammonia and warm water. Scrape off carefully with a wooden or plastic utensil.

Cleaning The Uncleanable... As a last resort, when dealing with those almost impossible marks like rust stains from screens or dried paint spatters, don a pair of rubber gloves and apply some oven cleaner to the window (not the panes!). Let it sit overnight and then wash off with your homemade window cleaner.

The Final Shine... A soft terry cloth is great for adding that extra shine.

Save On Paper Toweling... Use old crumpled newspaper to dry windows. The dyes in fresh newspaper are often not fully set and can sometimes mark your window and panes.

Cleaning Window Screens... Dip a paintbrush in kerosene and brush both sides of the screen. Dry with a clean cloth.

WINDOW DRESSINGS...

Cleaning Window Blinds... The "Homemade Window Cleaner" above is also great for cleaning vinyl blinds. If the weather's nice, take them down and lay them all out on something like an old plastic tablecloth and sponge them with the cleaner. Rinse them off with a hose and hang them on the clothesline to dry.

♦ If you don't want to take your venetian blinds down, get an old oven mitt and sprinkle fabric softener onto both sides of it. Now you'll find you can run the mitt between the blades and clean both the top and bottom at the same time!

♦ Wooden slatted blinds should not be wet too much when cleaning. Dampen a cloth with some warm water and dish soap. Wipe off with water-dampened cloth.

♦ Fabric blinds should be vacuumed carefully. I prefer to use a small handheld vacuum.

Cleaning Windowsills... A great windowsill cleaner is a mixture of one part rubbing alcohol to eight parts warm water.

Cleaning Window Sheers... A clever way to clean sheers and net curtains is to fill your bath with warm water and throw in a couple of denture tablets. Let the curtains sit overnight, then rinse well.

Cleaning Curtains... Most curtains can be laundered on a light cycle. Always check for colorfastness though.

♦ To add fullness to your drapes add ¾ cup Epsom salts to the final rinse cycle.

♦ On washable curtains, grease marks from hands can usually be taken out with a little waterless hand cleaner. Rinse with cool water.

Shrink-Free Curtains... There's nothing worse when washing curtains than having either the lining or the drapes shrinking disproportionately. So when washing your lined drapes, select the water temperature according to the fabric most likely to shrink...either the drapes or the lining.

Wrinkle-Free Curtains... Hang curtains up damp to avoid ironing them. Most wrinkles should fall out quickly.

Curtain Hang-Up... If you find when hanging curtains after you have just washed them that they don't hang evenly, try this trick. Take a broom handle or curtain rod and run it through the hem at the bottom of the curtain. The weight should straighten it out in no time.

Easy Drape "Dry Cleaning"... Place your drapes in the dryer with a damp towel. Select a delicate cycle for 15 to 20 minutes. Great for removing dust and generally freshening up the drapes' appearance.

♦ For a fresh fragrance, add a little fabric-softener liquid to the damp towel.

Don't Spare The Rod... When you remove your curtains for washing, make sure you take the opportunity to wipe the curtain rod down at the same time.

♦ You may want to apply a little talcum powder to the metal rod as well. This will help the curtain slide easier.

♦ For wooden rods, apply a little furniture polish.

~ ♦ ~

CHAPTER 7

ROUND ABOUT THE HOUSE

THE REST OF THE NOOKS AND CRANNIES!

THINGS THAT AREN'T NAILED DOWN

CLEANING ALPHABETICALLY...

Bedding... To kill off dust mites from bedding, place the item in a garbage bag. Leave the bag in your freezer for an hour or so.

Clever Candleholder Cleaning... Melted wax won't stick as easily to your candleholders if you rub them down first with a little petroleum jelly. It makes the cleanup a lot easier.

♦ You can also pour some water into the holder. Not only will it douse any flame when the candle burns down, but you should be able to remove the wax stub easily.

♦ You'll have less cleanup if the candle doesn't drip in the first place. Make your new candles dripless by soaking them in a strong saltwater solution for a few hours.

♦ Whiten yellowed white candles by rubbing them with ammonia.

Compact Discs... Clean your CDs with a soft, lint-free cloth. Make sure you wipe straight from the center out toward the edge of the disc.

Computer Keyboard Care... The first step to remember when cleaning your computer is to shut it off before you start cleaning.

♦ Remove dust by vacuuming with a soft-bristled brush attachment. If you wipe down the keys with a fabric softener sheet, it'll help to reduce that dust-attracting static.

♦ Greasy marks from fingers can often be cleaned off by wiping with a soft cloth dipped into some dena-tured alcohol.

Computer Mouse Care... Turn your computer off, unscrew the mouse-ball holder and remove the ball. Wipe the ball down with some rubbing alcohol. Using a cotton swab dipped in rubbing alcohol, clean the heads inside the mouse.

Doll Dilemma... To remove the odor from your kid's plastic doll, simply place it in a shopping bag with a few handfuls of cat litter. Leave it in there for 2 or 3 days.

Doll Dirt... For plastic dolls, you can usually rub off most marks with vegetable shortening.

♦ Remove marker or ink with a shot of hair spray. Check for colorfastness first.

Ebony Items... It's best to wipe ebony pieces with a mixture of equal parts vinegar, turpentine and boiled linseed oil. Use a soft cloth to apply and buff with.

Eyeglass Cleaner... Often hobbyists get various glues on the lenses of their eyeglasses. To remove, try wiping the lenses with ordinary acetone or certain nail-polish removers. Only use this method on glass lenses. Acetone products can dissolve plastic-based lenses.

Guitar Grit... To clean the inside of your guitar, simply throw a handful of raw rice into the guitar box and shake it up, baby!

Iron Deposits... Give your iron a cleaning every so often. Wipe the ironing surface down with some salt on a damp cloth and rinse off.

♦ For stubborn marks use some toothpaste and a soft cloth.

Ivory Items... Make a paste of 4 tablespoon natural yogurt and 3 teaspoon lemon juice. Apply with soft cloth, leave for 1 minute, then wipe off with damp cloth.

Lamp-Shade Cleaning... If a fabric lamp shade has dirty marks on it, the safest way to clean it is with a mixture of ½ cup dish soap, ½ teaspoon ammonia, 1 teaspoon vinegar and 1 quart of warm water. Use a hand mixer to froth the solution up and apply the foam only to the shade using a sponge. Wipe off with a damp cloth and dry immediately with a hair dryer set on cool.

♦ For most fabric lamp shades usually a light dusting with a soft-bristled paintbrush does the trick.

Laundry Hamper... Prevent that dirty-laundry-hamper odor by leaving a used fabric-softener sheet in it.

Mattress Maintenance... Once every 3 or 4 months or so, it's a good idea to sprinkle some baking soda onto your bed mattress. Leave it on for the day and then vacuum it off.

Needlework... Check for colorfastness, then wash with baby shampoo.

♦ For framed needlework, keep it out of direct sunlight to prevent fading. Clean by dusting gently with a feather duster.

Papier-Mâché Items... Blot carefully with a soft cloth dipped in cool water (stay away from any kind of soap). Sprinkle a little flour on the item and then brush off gently with a soft face brush.

Perking Up Those Covers... Spruce up your leather-bound books by rubbing a little petroleum jelly on the cover with a soft cloth. Buff well.

Perking Up Those Pages... To remove the musty odor from books that have been stored a long time, simply place the book in a paper bag and add a little baking soda. Shake it out well after 10 days or so.

♦ To remove mildew, sprinkle the pages with cornstarch, let sit 24 hours and dust off.

Pewter Pieces... Rub with a paste made from cigarette ash and olive oil. Buff well.

Piano Cleaning... Most pianos only need to be dusted lightly with a soft clean cloth. However you may want to vacuum the keyboard. Use the soft-brush attachment on your vacuum wand.

♦ To clean ivory keys, rub with a lemon half. Or use a paste of lemon juice and salt. Wipe off with a clean cloth.

♦ Or clean with a cloth moistened slightly with denatured alcohol. Wipe dry. Never use soap to clean ivory. It will stain.

♦ Plastic piano keys can usually be cleaned with a soft damp cloth. Buff dry with a dry cloth. If very grimy, buff with toothpaste on a soft cloth.

Picture Perfect... Wooden picture frames can be spruced up by polishing with a little matching shoe polish or some boiled linseed oil.

♦ Gilt picture frames need a little special attention when cleaning. Make a paste of 1 egg white and 1 level teaspoon baking soda. Using a soft cloth or sponge, dab the frame carefully to clean. If any residue remains, brush off with a soft brush like a shaving brush or face powder brush.

♦ When dusting oil paintings try using a silk cloth. It's very gentle on them.

♦ Watercolors and oil paintings can usually be cleaned by dabbing with a piece of bread.

Pillow Talk... Most foam, feather or down pillows and duvets can be washed in your washer on a cool, gentle wash setting, with a mild liquid soap. Foam pillows should be air-dried, while feather and down pillows can handle a tumbling in your drier, set on cool. Pop in a tennis ball or two to help fluff them up.

Plush Toys... To freshen up your kid's plush toys, give them a dry shampoo with some cornmeal. Rub in, let sit for an hour, then dust off, or vacuum gently.

♦ Or mix 3 tablespoons dish soap ¼ teaspoon ammonia and ¾ cup of water. Wisk the solution into a froth and apply the froth only to the toy. Wipe off with a damp cloth and allow it to air-dry.

♦ For stain removal on plush toys, wipe with the foam only from the following solution: ¼ cup water; ½ cup rubbing alcohol, ½ teaspoon dish soap. Beat to a froth with a hand mixer.

Portable Humidifier... Keep the drum clear of lime scale by adding ¼ cup white vinegar to the water reservoir every week it's in use.

Seashell And Coral Pieces...
Wash in hot water with a little water softener and dish soap added. Rinse well in cool water.

♦ To completely clean out fresh shells of any "tenants," bury the shells in the ground for a month or so. Mother Nature will do the rest.

Screen Gems... TV and computer screens can be dusted with used fabric-softener sheets or a soft cloth dipped into fabric softener. The antistatic properties help prevent dust being attracted to the screen surface.

♦ Remember not to clean your screens with any window or glass cleaners that have ammonia in them. It can sometimes cause damage to the finish that many manufacturers put on their screens.

Tablecloth Protection... Give your tablecloths a good shot of spray starch each time you wash them. You'll find they'll be less susceptible to staining.

Telephone Treatment... To bring a nice luster to your telephone's finish, try wiping it down with a little rubbing alcohol on a soft cloth.

♦ For stubborn, greasy buildup, wipe with a cloth dipped in ammonia.

Vases... To remove the stains caused by leftover flower water, fill the vase with hot water and add 5 capfuls of ammonia. Leave to sit for an hour or so and then rinse thoroughly with clean water. If stain persists, repeat and scour with the addition of 1 teaspoon dish soap.

♦ Or do as above but substitute the ammonia with 2 denture tablets.

♦ Liquid dishwasher detergent left overnight in the vase will usually remove most stains. Rinse with clean water.

Videotapes... It's best to use a good tape head cleaning cassette.

THINGS THAT ARE NAILED DOWN

CLEANING FIXTURES ALPHABETICALLY...

Brass Door Knockers... Ammonia usually cleans brass pretty well. Apply some to a soft cloth and rub the item gently.

◆ To prevent brass from tarnishing quickly, apply some car wax, lemon oil or even spray some furniture polish on.

◆ For more cleaning tips, see "Copper Pots."

Bronze Fittings... Buffing with some brown shoe polish on a soft cloth will give your bronze a pretty good protective finish.

◆ To clean bronze, wipe the item down with a little boiled linseed oil.

◆ Do not use ammonia on bronze. It usually contains copper and tin and the combination could damage the piece.

Ceiling Fans... To help prevent dust from sticking to your ceiling fan blades, buff them with hard car wax.

Chandelier Cleaning... Pour 4 tablespoons ammonia into ⅔ of a glass of white vinegar. Hold the glass over each individual crystal piece until it is totally immersed. Let drip-dry.

◆ You may want to place a drop cloth on the floor under the chandelier first. Or suspend an inverted golf umbrella under it.

Exhaust Fans... Apply a paste of water and baking soda to
the inside of your greasy kitchen exhaust fan. Let it sit for
an hour and rinse off with white vinegar.

◆   The filter can be soaked in a sink filled with
hot water and 1 cup of water softener.

Fireplace Facts... When sweeping ashes from a fireplace,
spread some used, wet coffee grounds on the ashes first.
This helps keep ash dust from spreading.

◆   To clean the face of your stone or
brick fireplace, scrub it with the
following solution: 2 cups distilled
white vinegar, 1 cup ammonia and
½ cup baking soda.

◆   For fireplace glass doors, apply a little oven cleaner
with a damp cloth to the cool window. Rinse off well
with clean water.

Furnace Humidifier... To clean
the sponge on the drum of your
furnace humidifier of lime scale
buildup, let it sit in a vinegar and
water solution. Use equal parts
white vinegar and water and let it
soak for about 3 hours. Rinse with
clean water.

Hot Water Heater... Clear hard-water deposits and sediment
from your water tank by letting a gallon or so of water out
of the tap at the bottom of the tank. Do this every season.

Louvered Doors... Dust between the louvers with a sock
stretched over a ruler. Apply a little furniture polish to the
sock first.

♦ Or dust off occasionally with a used fabric-softener
sheet.

Marble Mantelpiece Maintenance... For cleaning
and stain removal, try wiping with a damp rag
dipped into some borax. Rinse and dry immediately.
For more marble cleaning tips, see "Marble Floors."

♦ To add a protective finish to
your marble, try giving it a
light coat of paste wax and
buffing well.

Switch Plates... Clean light-
switch covers and plates with
a little baking soda on a
damp cloth.

Woodstove Wisdom... Clean woodstove windows easily by simply
dipping a wet rag into the wood ash
and rubbing it on the window.

♦ For really stubborn stains on
your woodstove window, do as
a friend of ours at the cottage
does. Spray a little oven cleaner
on a cloth. Then rub the cloth over the surface of the
cool window and leave it for 30 minutes or so. Wash off
with equal parts vinegar and water. Be sure to use
rubber gloves and be careful not to get the oven
cleaner on the door's gasket.

AND FINALLY…

ODORS ETC….

Musty Odors… To remove strong, musty odors from your home, you may need to hide it with a stronger fragrance. Oil of wintergreen on a few cotton puffs will often do just that.

Odors In General… Mix 1 cup of distilled white vinegar and ½ teaspoon peppermint extract. Fill a spray container or a plant mister with this solution and spray away those odors.

♦ Boil a small pot of water on the stove with a few tablespoons pure vanilla essence added.

♦ For a quick room deodorizer in the winter, pour a few drops of your favorite perfume or essential oil through the floor heat registers. When the furnace kicks in, the warm air will distribute the fragrance throughout the room.

Oven Cleaning Odor… To neutralize the odor from oven cleaner, bake several pieces of orange or lemon peel in the oven.

Varnish Hands… A handy alternative to paint thinner, when removing varnish or lacquer from your hands, is peanut butter.

~ ◆ ~

CHAPTER 8

WASH-DAY WISDOM

A LAUNDRY LIST OF SMART IDEAS!

LAUNDRY LOWDOWN

GENERAL LAUNDERING TIPS...

"Coin" Laundry... A good-working washer is important, but sometimes it breaks down and you can't afford a new one right away. Well, if you had placed a piggy bank on top of the washer and deposited $2 for each wash load, chances are you'd have enough money to buy a brand-new washer. It adds up quickly!

Washing The Washer... To keep your washer clean and fresh smelling, every so often let the tub fill with water and add 2 cups of white vinegar. Let the washer sit for an hour at that position, restart and allow it to go through its wash and rinse cycle. Then repeat the same process with 2 cups of bleach.

Washing The Laundry Tub... Apply a solution of 1 tablespoon ammonia, 1 tablespoon white vinegar, 1 teaspoon water softener (or washing soda) and ¾ cup warm water.

Temperature Control: Hot... (130°F/54°C) Use for washing whites, colorfasts, diapers and heavily soiled clothes.

Temperature Control: Warm... (100°F/37°C) Use for washing non-colorfasts, permanent press, knits, woolens, silk and mildly soiled clothes.

Temperature Control: Cold... (80°F/26°C, or less) Use for washing dark or bright colors, noncolorfast and lightly soiled clothes.

Washing Noncolorfast Garments... To help prevent colors running when washing new clothes, try adding about ¼ cup of salt to the laundry detergent when you put it in your washer.

♦ 1 teaspoon ammonia for every gallon of wash water can also do the trick.

♦ To set the colors in new cotton garments, soak them overnight in a solution of ½ cup distilled white vinegar, 1 tablespoon Epsom salts and 2 quarts of cold water.

Whiter Than White... To whiten your white socks and underwear, try boiling them in water, to which you've added a few slices of lemon or some lemon juice.

♦ Perk up those faded white garments by soaking them for about $\frac{1}{2}$ hour in the following solution: 1 gallon warm water, 2 tablespoons ammonia, 4 tablespoons dishwasher detergent and 4 tablespoons ordinary dish soap. Launder garments as usual.

♦ Or soak them in 1 cup of baking soda mixed into a pail of warm water and leave overnight before washing.

♦ Stained handkerchiefs will often come cleaner if you soak them first in salt water.

White Linen... To perk up and whiten yellowed linen, pour a melted bar of white soap into a pail of milk. Let it sit in the solution for an hour or so and then wash by hand and rinse well with clean water.

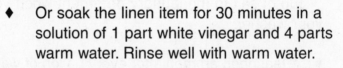 ♦ Or soak the linen item for 30 minutes in a solution of 1 part white vinegar and 4 parts warm water. Rinse well with warm water.

White Lace... To whiten your lace items that have yellowed, mix $\frac{1}{4}$ p baking soda, 1 tablespoon laundry detergent and 4 cups of water. Bring the solution to a boil, remove from the heat and dip the items into the hot liquid. Make sure you wear gloves, or use tongs. That water will be really hot!

Lint-Free Laundry... Add $\frac{1}{2}$ cup white vinegar to the rinse cycle.

♦ Sometimes a rubber dish-washing glove will remove lint after the fact.

Damage Control... It's a good idea to turn your clothes inside out when laundering. Not only will any washer damage be kept on the inside, but it will also extend the life of your clothes by reducing washing wear and tear.

Softening The Load... Instead of buying expensive fabric-softener sheets, simply throw a $\frac{1}{2}$ cup of baking soda into the washer with your laundry detergent. It works pretty well.

♦ You can also make your own fabric softener and save yourself some money. Mix 2 cups white vinegar with 2 cups baking soda. While it's fizzing, add 4 cups cold water. Pour about $\frac{1}{4}$ cup into your washer's final rinse cycle.

♦ Or pour a few drops of fabric-softener liquid onto an old facecloth and throw that into the dryer along with the load. It's much cheaper than the sheets, not to mention, of course, that much better for the environment.

♦ Remember, if your water is very hard, you may need to add more detergent than normal to obtain enough suds.

Errant Shoelaces... Wash your shoelaces in the washer along with the rest of the wash. But tie them through shirt buttonholes first. This way you'll know where they are!

Errant Socks... Keep a small basket on your dryer to keep odd socks in. As their mates come out of the Bermuda Triangle (dryer), you'll be able to match them with the socks on hand.

SPECKS, SPOTS AND SPILLS

STAIN REMOVAL ALPHABETICALLY...

NB: All stain-removal hints apply to <u>washable</u> fabrics only. Always check the stain-removing solution for colorfastness on an inconspicuous area first.

General Stain Strategy... First things first. Remove as much of the spill with a paper towel or spatula as soon as possible. Stains are much easier to remove before they get a chance to set.

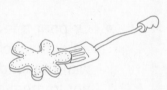

♦ It's usually best to use a dabbing motion rather than a rubbing one.

♦ Also, work from the outside in when applying solutions. This helps contain the stain as it's dissolved.

♦ It's best to use cold water on nongreasy stains. Generally, hot water tends to set the stain.

♦ If you are unsure of the stain, or it is made up of both greasy and nongreasy stains, always treat as a nongreasy stain first.

Adhesives... See "Glue."

Baby Spit-Ups... Wet the stained area thoroughly with water. Work a layer of powdered dishwasher deter-gent into the wet stain and leave for 12 hours or so. Launder as usual.

Bacon Splatters... Simply rub the stain well with water-less hand cleaner and a little dish soap. Rinse off in tepid water.

Ballpoint-Pen Ink... See "Ink."

Beer... Soak the item in a solution of 2 cups cool water and ¼ cup white distilled vinegar.

♦ Or dab the area with some glycerin as a laundry prewash.

♦ For stubborn stains on whites, blot with a weak solution of 1 tablespoon hydrogen peroxide and ½ cup cool water.

Blood... If it's just a small drop of your own blood, try sucking the stain out. Often your own saliva does the trick!

♦ Or apply a paste of baking soda and cold water. Let sit until dry and rinse off.

♦ Some people swear by ammonia, especially for their white fabrics. Just a small amount though; it's very strong.

♦ Waterless hand cleaner works too! Simply rub the stain well and rinse in tepid water.

♦ For really stubborn or old bloodstains, soak the area in some hydrogen peroxide.

♦ If the stain is on silk or satin, it's best to have it professionally cleaned. However, sometimes, depending on the specific type of fabric, you can try applying a paste of powdered laundry starch and cold water. Let dry and brush away.

Butter And Margarine... See "Grease."

♦ Also, giving the item a quick wash in a little biodegradable liquid soap and very hot water can often do the trick.

Candle Wax... Place 2 folded paper towels on both sides of the stained area and press with a medium warm iron. Do not move the iron while applying. The paper towel will absorb the melted wax. Replace the paper towel and continue. Repeat until the stain is gone. Check garment often to make sure the fabric is not being scorched.

♦ If there is a residual mark from colored die, you can usually remove it with a little paint thinner or rubbing alcohol. Launder as usual.

♦ Often you can simply chip the wax off with your fingers, if you leave the garment in the freezer for a few hours first.

Chocolate... Remove any excess chocolate first, then immediately run some club soda through the fabric and rinse with a mild detergent and cold water. If the stain persists, follow up with a mixture of 1 tablespoon ammonia and 1 cup cold water. Dab the solution on the fabric working from the outside in. Rinse well and wash the item as usual.

♦ Waterless hand cleaner also works well to remove those nasty chocolate stains!

♦ If you prefer, you can apply some glycerin, let it sit for an hour or two, then wash in cold water and a little borax.

♦ Often, just simply soaking the item in a solution of 1 part water softener and 8 parts cool water does the trick.

Cigarette Ashes... These can often be removed by rubbing with a little waterless hand cleaner and dish soap. Rinse well in tepid water.

Coffee... Apply waterless hand cleaner. Rinse off with cool water.

♦ Apply a paste of equal parts glycerin and borax, let sit for an hour or two, then rinse in cold water.

♦ Or, soak the item in 1 tablespoon 3% hydrogen peroxide and ¾ cup cool water.

♦ You may also want to try a quick wash in cold water and then a white vinegar rinse afterward. Rinse again in cold water.

Collar Rings…. See "Perspiration."

♦ Or mix a paste of baking soda and white vinegar in a bowl and apply to the collar ring while the mixture is still fizzing. Let it sit for 1 hour and then launder as usual.

Crayon… See candle-wax hint with paper towels. Waterless hand cleaner rubbed into the mark may also work. Sometimes hair spray as well.

♦ Or remove as much of the excess as possible, then rub in a mixture of equal parts baby oil, petroleum jelly and glycerin. Wash in hot water. If there are residual grease stains, apply waterless hand cleaner and rinse with water.

♦ Sometimes crayon marks can be removed by rubbing them with some ordinary shortening. Launder as usual.

♦ As a last resort, you can try rubbing the garment with a little paint thinner and then putting it through a regular hot-water wash cycle together with a cup of baking soda.

Curry... Good luck! Here are a few things you can try. First, try rubbing the stain with a mixture of 3 tablespoons glycerin, 4 tablespoons water and 1 tablespoon ammonia. Let it sit for an hour, then launder it in warm water.

◆ Waterless hand cleaner works on certain curry stains. Give it a shot.

Deodorant Marks... To easily remove those unsightly white deodorant lines from your dark tops, simply rub them off with panty hose. It works great.

Egg... If a cold-water wash doesn't remove the stain, you can try this. Fill a cup ¼ full of baking soda, add another ¼ cup of glycerin and top up the cup with cool water. Apply the mixture to the stained garment and then wash as normal.

◆ Or try waterless hand cleaner and a little ordinary dish soap. Simply rub the stain well and rinse out in tepid water.

 ◆ Dried, older marks can sometimes be removed by soaking for 1 hour or 2 in 1 part hydrogen peroxide and 6 parts cold water.

Fruit... Mix ¼ cup baking soda, 1 tablespoon borax and ½ cup cool water. Apply the mixture to the stain and leave for 20 minutes or so. Rinse off with cool water.

♦ Stubborn fruit stains may have to be soaked for an hour or two in equal parts hydrogen peroxide and cold water.

♦ Sometimes, if you leave the garment in milk overnight, it will remove the stain.

♦ Or soak in equal parts glycerin and cool water for 2 to 3 hours. Rinse out with clean water.

♦ If you catch the stain immediately, lemon juice rubbed on may do the trick. Leave in sun to dry.

Fruit-Juice Stains... Many fruit-juice stains can be treated as you would treat fruit stains. However, here are some tips specifically for fruit juice.

♦ Rinse the stain in cool water, then dab with denatured alcohol.

♦ Soak the garment in a solution of 2 tablespoons borax in 1 cup of cold water for 1 hour or 2.

Glue... Epoxy glue and superglue can often be removed from clothing by dabbing with some lighter fluid or denatured alcohol.

♦ If you're not sure of the type of glue you want to remove, you may have to experiment with the following treatments. One at a time, of course!

    1) Acetone
    2) Paint thinner
    3) 1 part ammonia and 4 parts cool water.
    4) Nail-polish remover
    5) Eucalyptus oil

Grass... Really persistent grass stains can often be removed by soaking in a solution of 2 tablespoon rubbing alcohol, 1 tablespoon glycerin and $\frac{1}{4}$ cup warm water for 30 to 60 minutes.

♦ Often a little sponging with denatured alcohol will do the trick. Rinse well with water.

♦ Another method is to apply a paste of cream of tartar and water. Let the garment sit for 5 minutes and rinse out.

♦ Or mix $\frac{1}{4}$ teaspoon ammonia with 1 teaspoon hydrogen peroxide and apply it to stain. Rinse well with cool water.

Gravy... First, try washing the stain with warm water and dish soap.

♦ If the stain still persists, try dabbing it with a solution of $\frac{1}{2}$ cup water, $\frac{1}{2}$ teaspoon ammonia and $\frac{1}{2}$ teaspoon iodized salt.

Grease... Waterless hand cleaner, rubbed into the stain with your finger or a toothbrush, usually works very well. Rinse in clean water.

♦ Mix 1 part salt with 4 parts rubbing alcohol and apply to the stain.

♦ Or spread a paste of water softener, borax and water over the area. Leave for an hour then wash in hot water. If you don't have any water softener or borax on hand, you can try applying a paste of baking soda and water.

♦ On delicates, try washing the item with regular baby shampoo and hot water, to which you've added 1 tablespoon glycerin.

♦ A tip grandma used to use and, believe it or not, many people still swear by, is lard. Rub some into the stain and then wash with hot soapy water.

Gum... To remove stuck gum from clothing, simply place the item in your freezer compartment for an hour or so. This will usually harden the gum enough to allow you to dislodge it easily.

♦ Any residue can often be removed by soaking the area in white vinegar overnight.

♦ Rubbing alcohol often loosens up the residue too. Use a toothbrush.

Hair Dye... Often a shot of hair spray will loosen hair-coloring stains. Best to catch it fresh.

♦ If the dye is on your skin, an old hairdresser's trick is to use a little wet dye to remove the dried dye. Wash the wet dye off your skin immediately though!

Hamburger Juice... Rub with waterless hand cleaner, then rinse with tepid water.

Homemade Spot Remover... Here's how to make your own commercial spot remover. Simply mix $\frac{1}{2}$ cup rubbing alcohol, $\frac{1}{2}$ cup water and 1 teaspoon dish soap. It's as simple as that!

 ♦ It's a good idea to place a sponge under the garment when using your spot remover. It contains the solution and prevents the garment from moving as you treat it.

Ink... A great way of removing ballpoint-ink stains is to use hair spray (pump or aerosol). Douse the stain with the hair spray and then rub with a bar of soap. Rinse the garment in cold water. Remember hot water can set nongreasy stains.

♦ Rubbing alcohol dabbed on the stained area may also lift the ink.

♦ Or mix up a paste of cream of tartar and lemon juice. Smear over the stain and let sit for an hour or so. Launder in cool water.

Iodine... First, wash with cool water and dish soap. If the stain persists, dab with denatured alcohol.

♦ Waterless hand cleaner works too! Simply rub the stain well and rinse in tepid water.

Jam... See "Fruit."

♦ Or soak in a solution of biodegradable soap and water.

Juice... See "Fruit."

Ketchup... See "Tomato-Based Stains."

Lipstick... Hair spray usually works very well. Douse the area well and rub hard with a bar of hand or laundry soap. Launder as usual.

♦ Another method of removing lipstick stains from shirts and blouses is to blot the area with a little denatured alcohol.

 ♦ Or dab with baking soda and lemon juice. Wash as normal.

♦ Rub in equal parts petroleum jelly and glycerin. Wash in hot soapy water.

♦ As a last resort, dab on some paint thinner. Follow up with a little dish soap and then launder the garment in hot water.

Makeup... Apply hair spray and treat as for lipstick stain above.

♦ Sometimes, cornstarch rubbed into the stain and left to sit for an hour or so does the trick.

♦ Remove as much as possible with a paper towel. Then soak the area in a solution of 1 tablespoon ammonia and 2 cups of cool water.

♦ Most eye makeup on clothing can be removed with waterless handcleaner. Rinse well. Launder per label instructions.

Marker... Very often, most marker stains can be removed by spraying the area with hair spray. Rub hard with a bar of hand soap and rinse in cold water. Launder as usual.

Medicine... As a general rule of thumb, you should be able to remove most medicine spills by simply laundering in a cool wash. However, for those persistent stains, blot the item with denatured alcohol first and then rinse in clean water.

Mildew... For brightly colored garments try the simple route first. Take a bar of laundry soap and rub the bar hard into the stain. Let it sit in direct sunlight for an hour or two. Rinse with clean water.

♦ Another method is to apply a paste of borax and water.

♦ Or dampen the stain with powdered laundry starch, salt and lemon juice and let it sit out in the sun for a while.

♦ Often a weak solution of water and ammonia works. Sponge with vinegar afterward and leave to dry in the sun.

♦ You can also dab the stain with some hydrogen peroxide and launder as usual.

Motor Oil And Grease... We've found that using waterless hand cleaner as a prewash will work on most oil and grease stains.

♦ Or if it's really bad, soak the garment in cola overnight.

 ♦ And to get rid of that oil odor, throw a cup of baking soda into the wash cycle.

Mud... Slice a raw potato in half and rub the mud stain. Soak the item in cool water for one hour, then launder as usual.

♦ For the stubborn variety, soak the stain in a solution of 2 cups warm water, ½ cup borax and ½ cup baking soda for 1 hour or 2.

Mustard... The first thing to try is rubbing with waterless hand cleaner. Rinse in cold water.

 ♦ You can also soak the item for 2 hours in white vinegar. Then wash the item in cold water while rubbing with a bar of laundry soap. Soak 12 hours in the soapy water. If necessary, you can use a mild bleach solution.

♦ Or apply rubbing alcohol and launder the clothing as usual.

♦ A little glycerin applied to the stain may also do the trick.

♦ Another method is to soak the stain in equal parts water and hydrogen peroxide.

Nail Polish... Sponge the area with acetone or nail-polish remover with acetone in it (the nonoily type). Work with a dabbing motion from the outside of the stain toward the center to contain it. Launder in cool water and detergent. Several applications may be necessary.

♦ Or dab the area with denatured alcohol. Rinse off with cool water.

♦ For really stubborn nail-polish stains, try spraying the stain with oven cleaner. Let it sit for an hour or two, put your rubber gloves on and rub the stain with a toothbrush. Launder as usual. This is a pretty drastic method, so use it only as a last resort on really durable fabrics.

Nicotine... To remove stains, blot the area with some eucalyptus oil. Launder as usual.

Paint... To remove dried paint from washable fabric, try this. Rub shortening into the mark and leave it overnight. The next day, scrub the mark with a stiff brush. When the paint has been removed, rub some waterless hand cleaner into the area and rinse it well in warm water. This part of the process should take out any oily residue from the shortening.

♦ For oil paint, mix 2 tablespoons ammonia and 1 tablespoon turpentine. Rub the solution into the stain and launder in warm water. Several applications may be necessary.

♦ For really stubborn dried-on oil and latex paint, spray some oven cleaner on and let it sit on the item for 3 or 4 hours. Wearing rubber gloves, rub well with a stiff brush and wash with hot water and dish soap. Launder as usual. Use this method only on durable, washable fabrics.

♦ Waterless hand cleaner rubbed into the stain often does the trick. The older the stain, the longer you leave it on before laundering.

♦ Delicate items need special treatment. Try mixing together ¼ cup white distilled vinegar, 4 tablespoons glycerin and ½ cup warm water. Rub the mixture into the mark carefully and knead the garment gently to loosen the paint. Launder as usual.

Perfume... For stubborn perfume stains, mix some glycerin and water of equal proportions and blot the area well. Let sit for 2 hours or so and then wash in cool, mild soapy water.

♦ Or sponge some paint thinner onto the stain and rinse off immediately with some dish soap and cold water.

♦ Ammonia often works too. Blot the area first and then wash in some cold water and a little dish soap.

Perspiration... Place the garment in a bucket of warm water with 1 cup of vinegar and ¼ cup salt. Soak for about an hour before laundering.

♦ Or soak the garment in a solution of 2 tablespoons cream of tartar and 1 gallon warm water for about an hour. Launder as usual.

♦ Another method is to apply a paste of water softener and water to the area. Rub hard with a bar of laundry soap.

♦ You can try soaking the stain in a solution of ½ cup warm water and 2 powdered aspirins for 2 or 3 hours.

♦ As a last resort, soak the area in equal parts of hydrogen peroxide and warm water for an hour or so. Launder as normal.

Pet Accidents... First, pour club soda on the area and let it soak while you mix the following solution: 1 cup hydrogen peroxide, 1 teaspoon dish soap and 1 tablespoon baking soda. This should remove the stain as well as the odor. Due to its volatility, you should throw out the solution immediately after using.

♦ Or soak the stain in a solution of ¼ cup ammonia in 2 cups of water for 5 minutes. Rinse in some white vinegar and then launder as usual.

Pop... See "Fruit."

♦ Or blot with equal parts denatured alcohol and white vinegar.

♦ Another method you can try is to dab the area with rubbing alcohol. Let sit for 15 minutes, repeat if necessary. Launder as usual.

Red Wine... Red-wine stains usually literally disappear from washable fabrics if you dip them into a solution of 1 tablespoon borax and 2 cups warm water.

 ♦ Another method of treating a wine stain immediately is to sprinkle salt liberally over the area to absorb the spill. Or soak the area with club soda and blot with paper towels.

♦ If stain persists, or for older stains, you can try dabbing the area with a little hydrogen peroxide. Dab/rinse with cold water.

 ♦ Or wet the stained area well with water. Then spread equal parts baking soda and borax on the area. Leave for 30 minutes, then rinse.

♦ You may also want to try our friend's method. Soak the stain in glycerin for an hour or two. Rinse it in cold water, then dab the stained area with denatured alcohol.

Rust... Remove rust from clothing or fabrics by applying a paste of lemon juice and baking soda. Let sit for an hour, then hang outside in the sun to dry.

♦ Or cover the area with cream of tartar. Roll the item tightly and soak it in a bucket of hot water. Launder as usual.

Salad Dressing... See "Grease."

 ♦ The easiest way to remove oily salad-dressing stains, in fact most greasy stains for that matter, is to rub the area well with water-less hand cleaner. Rinse with cold water.

Sap... To remove tree sap, blot the area with a little lighter fluid. Launder immediately.

♦ If the sap is on your skin, it can usually be removed by rubbing with acetone or an acetone-based nail-polish remover.

 Scorch... Dampen a piece of cloth with a weak solution of hydrogen peroxide and press the cloth over the scorched area with a medium-heat iron.

♦ Often, a soaking in a mixture of ¼ cup borax and 4 cups of water will do the trick. Rinse well.

♦ Or mix ¼ cup borax, 2 cups cold water and ¼ cup glycerin. Let the mark soak in the solution for about half an hour, kneading the fabric every 5 minutes or so. Launder as usual.

♦ As a last resort, mix 1 cup of distilled white vinegar with ½ cup baby powder. Cut 3 onions in half, add them to the mixture and bring to a boil. Let cool and dab the area with the solution.

Self-Tanning Lotion... Simply dab the area with some hydrogen peroxide and launder as usual.

Shiny Fabric... If the fabric is not too worn, you can sometimes remove the shine by rubbing the area with half a raw potato. Let it dry completely and brush briskly with a clothes brush.

Shoe Polish... You can often remove shoe polish from clothing by dabbing the marked area with equal parts ammonia and water. Rinse well in warm water and a little ordinary dish soap.

♦ Sponge with denatured alcohol. Rinse with warm water.

♦ Or try dabbing the area with some turpentine on a sponge. Wash afterward with a little dish soap and warm water.

Soot... Shake off excess, then lightly rub some talcum powder onto the stain. Launder as usual.

Sorbet... See "Fruit."

Soup... See "Grease."

Soy Sauce... See "Tomato-Based Stains."

♦ You may want to try washing the garment in cool water with a little ordinary dish soap.

Spaghetti Sauce... See "Tomato-Based Stains."

Spirits... See "White Wine" and "Beer."

Suntan Lotion... See "Grease."

Syrup... See "Fruit."

♦ Or soak in a solution of biodegradable soap and water.

Tar... First place the garment in the freezer for 2 hours or so. You should then be able to chip off most of the brittle, excess tar. The next step is to mix 2 tablespoon butter and 2 tablespoon eucalyptus oil and work it well into the stain. Finally rub in some regular dish soap and rinse the item in warm water.

♦ If you don't have any eucalyptus oil, try substituting it with a little paint thinner, but remember to work on the stain from the outside in, to contain it. Launder as usual.

Tea... Waterless hand cleaner works well for tea stains. Simply rub it well into the stain and rinse it off with cold water.

♦ Soak the area in a solution of 1 part borax and 8 parts cold water for an hour or so. Then launder the item as usual.

Tobacco... See "Nicotine."

Tomato-Based Stains... For ketchup- and spaghetti-sauce-type stains, rub waterless hand cleaner on and rinse in cold water.

♦ Or soak the stain in a solution of 1 part hydrogen peroxide and 6 parts water. Launder the garment normally.

Typing Correction Fluid... Often these marks can be removed by simply blotting the area with some acetone. Regular acetone-based nail-polish remover can also work well.

♦ Paint thinner can also be successful on certain fabrics. You may want to wash the paint thinner smell out with warm water after this treatment with some dish soap and a little lemon juice.

♦ Alternatively, pour a little rubbing alcohol into a small bowl and soak the stain in it for an hour or so. Rinse off with cool water.

Urine... See "Pet Accidents" recipe.

♦ Or mix 1 part ammonia with 10 parts water and allow the garment to soak for about half an hour in the mixture. Then wash in a solution of hot water and dish soap.

Vomit... First, remove as much of the excess deposit as possible. Then wash the stain in a mixture of 1 tablespoon biodegradable soap, ¼ cup white vinegar and ½ cup warm water. Launder the item as usual.

◆ Try rubbing with waterless hand cleaner if the stain persists. Rinse in cool water.

◆ Soak in a solution of 1 tablespoon borax and 2 cups warm water. For tough stains, soak overnight. Launder as usual.

◆ To remove the odor, pour 1 cup table salt into a bucket of warm water. Soak the garment in it for 1 hour. Launder as usual.

Watermarks... If you're concerned about causing watermarks on your fabric when removing other marks or stains, simply pour a little baby powder on the wet area. Position a paper towel over the powder and then place an iron set on medium heat on top until the area is dry. In most cases, this should do the trick.

Wax... See "Candle Wax."

White Wine... Remove white-wine stains by dabbing the area with a little white vinegar. Rinse well in cool water before laundering.

Wine... See "White Wine" and "Red Wine."

Won't Come Out At All!... There comes a time when you've tried everything to remove that stain, but to no avail. When this happens it's time to work around it rather than on it! Here are a few clever ideas to help you do just that:

♦ When stains are on a visible area, simply cover them with a broach or a badge/button.

♦ In other spots, a belt or even a scarf can do the trick.

♦ If the stain's on an elbow or a knee, it can usually be hidden with a fashionable patch that can be simply ironed on.

♦ A stain on a long-sleeved shirt can become no stain on a short-sleeved shirt.

♦ Many light garments can be easily dyed to hide the stain.

♦ Another clever idea is to embroider a creative design over the stain with different colored threads.

♦ If you have an artistic flair, you could paint a design over the stain with fabric paint.

~ ♦ ~

CHAPTER 9

REGROUP AND REORGANIZE

PUTTING CLUTTER IN ITS PLACE, ROOM BY ROOM!

THE ENTRANCE HALL

THE FIRST THING YOU SEE...

Knickknack Container... Place a large decorative ceramic bowl or straw basket on a small table in your entrance hall. It comes in handy for dropping off small items like your keys, gloves, etc. when you come home. They'll be there, ready and waiting for you, when you go out again.

Closet Hang Ups... String two lengths of cord on the inside of your hall closet and attach several clothespins along each string. When the kids come in they can pin their mittens together on the lower string and their hats on the upper string. As a result, you not only will know where they are, you'll also know that they're drying as they're hanging up.

♦ Or suspend a shoe bag on the inside of the door. The compartments are great for mitts, hats, etc. You can even keep a pair of slippers in one of the pockets to slip on when removing wet shoes.

Closet Smarts... Part of being organized is to make sure that items are conveniently accessible. For example, the reason you keep your coats in the entrance-hall closet is because that's where you need them the most...when you leave. Apply the same rule to things like walking sticks, rain shoes, keys, etc.

Tip For A Rainy Day... Keep those umbrella's from cluttering up your entrance hall closet. Get a two-foot piece of 6-inch clay water pipe and place it on one of those clay plant-pot dishes. It makes a really neat umbrella stand.

THE LIVING ROOM

WHERE YOU SIT...

Neatness Is In The Eye Of The Beholder... Here are some clever time-saving tricks to use to give the impression your living room is cleaner and tidier than it might really be.

♦ Make sure your light-colored chairs are clean; your guests will automatically think the darker ones are clean too!

♦ A couple of colorful vases of fresh flowers will usually distract the eye from all but the most obvious untidiness.

♦ Comb out the fringes on your carpets and area rugs to give the impression of neatness.

Magazine Mayhem... In order to avoid piles of magazines cluttering the room, cut out the features you feel are important to you and keep them in a shoe box in the cupboard or in your recipe area. Dispose of the magazines quickly before you change your mind!

In The Front, Out The Back... Make a strict policy that whenever you buy anything new, an item of equal size must go out from that room.

♦ You can also apply the "one in four rule." For every new item, four old items of any size or from any room must go.

Card Clutter... Decide how long you really want to keep those birthday or Mother's Day cards on the mantel. Throw away the cards that don't hold exceptional sentimental value to you or your family.

Paper Trail... When you've read your mail, or the kid's school notes, immediately file them in their designated folders, or transfer the information into your diary, computer or onto your calendar.

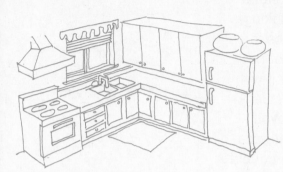

THE
KITCHEN

COOKING UP SOME NEAT STORAGE IDEAS...

Saving Energy... It makes sense to arrange your storage so that everything is kept as close as possible to where you're going to use it the most.

Under Your Nose... Store items like salt, flour, sugar, spaghetti, etc. in attractive glass containers on your open shelves or counter. This way you won't find untidy boxes left out to clutter up the counter.

♦ Do the same with your spices. You'll also use them more often this way.

Basket Case... If small items like matches, toothpicks, etc. are driving you crazy by filling up your kitchen drawers, here's an answer. Decorate an apple or tomato basket with some paint and ribbon, pop the offending items in it and keep it out of the way, on top of a reachable cupboard or shelf.

Steamer Storage... Get double duty out of your large bamboo steamer. Store your onions or potatoes in it while it's not in use. The air flow will help your veggies last longer too!

(Fun)due Pot... If you never use that fondue pot that's been taking up valuable space in the cupboard, get rid of it and replace it with cookware you actually use. However, if you do actually use it occasionally, let it do double duty in the meantime.  Place it on an open shelf and use it to store small kitchen items or even display it on top of the cupboard with a nice plant in it.

In-Wall Pantry... A clever way to store your canned and bottled goods is in the wall! Get a handyperson to cut out a 3-foot-high piece of wallboard between one or two of your wall studs and install some 4-inch shelves.

Bench Storage... When you buy your next kitchen table set, buy benches instead of chairs. They take up less space and many of them are made with a storage area under the seat. Great for items like tablecloths, napkins, recipe books, etc.

Place-Mat Storage... Save drawer space by clamping your place mats and folded tablecloths in sets with pants hangers. Hang them up inside your pantry or kitchen cupboard door.

Recipe Books... Often there is a lot of wasted space between the top of your kitchen counter and the bottom of your kitchen cupboards. Why not attach a shelf there and store your recipe books on and under it.

Recipe Records... Pick up an old computer at a garage sale. Paint it to match your kitchen décor and set it up on a counter in the corner. Now you can transfer all those recipes you cut out from magazines, etc., onto your computer. It's also convenient to read the recipe right off the screen when cooking. You may even want to gradually enter your favorite recipes from your recipe books and categorize them to suit yourself.

Appliance Storage... If you can see your appliances, you're more likely to use them. Instead of an appliance "garage," dedicate a set of shelves (my sister uses a set of room-divider shelves between her cooking area and the kitchen table) to store your small appliances. This way you'll also be able to tell which ones you actually use and which ones can eventually be disposed of.

Herb Storage... Herbs need to be kept away from heat and light, so why not store them in one of your kitchen drawers near, but not right at, the stove. If you lay them flat you'll be able to read the labels easily.

♦ Or get one of those see-through shoe bags. Cut it into two pieces that will match the size of two of your cupboard doors and attach them on the inside. The pockets are just the right size for herbs and sauces, etc.

Counter Space Saver... When you're running out of counter space when preparing a large meal, here's a neat trick. Simply place a breadboard on top of an open drawer. More counter space!

Cupboard Space Saver... To maximize space in your glassware cupboard, arrange alternate glasses upside down.

THE BEDROOM

MAKING YOUR BED(ROOM)...

Make Your Bed... Get into the habit of making your bed as soon as you get out of it. Procrastination often leads to an untidy bedroom.

Bedside Buildup... If your bedside tabletop is beginning to get a little overcrowded, here's a solution. Suspend one of those shoe bags with all the pockets on them behind and just above the bedside table. It's great for holding stuff like small books, reading glasses, pill bottles, tissues, even a portable phone.

Under The Bed... If you're stuck for storage space for your seasonal clothing, fold them well and place them in several boxes under the bed. The clear plastic types are best, so you can see what's in them. Most beds are high enough to keep boxes under them.

Trunk Tip... An old steamer trunk or blanket box placed at the bottom of your bed is ideal for storing seasonal clothing and extra linen. It also can be an attractive feature, not to mention the convenience of sitting on it to tie your shoelaces!

Less Is More... Cut down on closet overcrowding by gradually replacing many of your colored and patterned clothes with black clothes. They're far more versatile and you can brighten your outfit with colored or patterned accessories, such as scarves, jewelry or belts, etc.

Model Behavior... It's sometimes easier to throw out seldom-used clothes if you model them for yourself. If they don't fit anymore or are totally out of style, it'll show!

Top-Floor Storage... For items you don't use too often, the top of your wardrobe provides an excellent storage facility. Painted boxes or even decorated baskets can be filled and placed there out of the way and still match the décor.

♦ If your wardrobe has a high enough top railing, you can store flat suitcases up there, filled with all sorts of things.

Sweater Storage... Sweaters should preferably be stored flat, either on shelves or in drawers. However, if you're stacking them, they'll look better when you wear them if you store the lighter-weight ones on top. Don't stack them too high, or they'll lose their shape.

Clever Closet Tips...
Peg your scarves on clothes hangers and hang them in the closet, rather than jam them into drawers. They're easier to see and won't wrinkle.

♦ Attach a multipocketed shoe organizer to the inside of one of your closet doors. Add a few hooks on another door for belts.

♦ Often there's room to install one more shelf between the top shelf and the top of the closet. This lofty storage space comes in handy for storing items that are seldom used.

♦ Hang short items like blouses, etc., along one half of the closet rod. This leaves room to place a small chest of drawers directly underneath the hanging clothes and out of the way.

♦ Group items together in your closet. Keep the same colors together as well as the same functions. For example, work clothes, casual clothes, formal clothes, etc.

Scarf Organizer... Save the cardboard centers from paper towels, etc., and wrap your scarves around them. No more fold marks!

♦ Hang your scarves in your closet with their matching outfits instead of tucking them away, out of sight and out of mind.

Drawer Storage... To help keep drawers tidy, place several small open boxes in the drawer to act as compartments.

♦ Save your empty toilet rolls and place them upright in your hosiery drawer. Store your different colored panty hose and tights in them. To stop them from falling over, secure them in groups of four with a rubber band.

Jewelry Organizer... Make a nice big padded frame from an existing picture frame with some matching fabric, stuffing and a little glue. Place a favorite photograph in the frame and stick all your broaches and pins around it. A great storage unit as well as a really funky picture frame.

♦ A great jewelry organizer is one of those see-through plastic bags with tiny pockets. They often come with a hanger attached, in order to hang on your closet rod.

◆ An inexpensive jewelry organizer for your small pieces is an ordinary egg carton. Keep it out of sight in your drawer.

◆ An old antique candelabra makes a clever holder for necklaces, bracelets and chains, not to mention an interesting feature to your dresser.

THE KIDS' ROOM

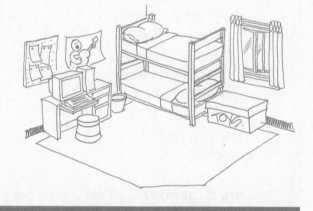

KIDZ KLUTTER...

Seasonal Storage... Buy a cheap plastic garbage can and fill it with your children's out-of-season clothing. Replace the lid with a square or round piece of wood and drape it with a matching piece of fabric. Add a little lamp and you have an attractive corner storage table.

♦ Or simply hang a second closet rod below the level of the clothes on the upper rod. Attach it in place with two ropes, one at either end, tied to the upper rod. Hang your child's in-season clothes on the lower rod. This way he can learn to hang up his own clothes, at his own level.

A Little Bribery... Give the kids a few good-size boxes and tell them to put all the toys they don't want into the boxes. Offer to pay $10 a box into their savings accounts. Charity gets the toys, your kids get rich and you get organized!

Toy Hang Ups... Attach one of those shoe bags with compartments to the back of the door, or inside the closet. They are great for storing toys like small dolls, stuffed animals, motorcars, etc.

Toy-Box Blues... Instead of throwing all the toys into one large toy box, pack them according to their type in clear plastic boxes. Slip them out of the way, under the bed if possible. This makes it easy for the child to identify the toy he wants, without him strewing all the toys on the floor first.

♦ Or buy an inexpensive plastic garbage can. As colorful as you can get. Get your child to decorate it with his own graffiti and stickers and you'll find he's more likely to use it.

Lego Logic... Take a circular piece of heavy cloth about 4–5 feet in diameter and hem the circumference. Run a heavy string or light rope through the hem. Now the child can use the cloth as a rug upon which to set up the Lego. When finished, simply pull the string tight and it forms a great storage bag for those errant Lego pieces.

Hatbox Heaven... If you're on the lookout for clever storage containers, do as my sister does. She came up with a great space-saving idea for her daughter's room: using decorative hatboxes. They're wonderful for storing under-garments, socks, scarves, etc. She just stacked them together to make an attractive feature in the room. Cake and cookie tins work well too.

THE BASEMENT

STORING BELOW...

Boxing Day... Make every day a boxing day. Keep good strong boxes in your basement or storage area and as you find things lying around that you aren't using that much, but still need, pop them into a box. Identify each box with a number and write down in a "master" book the rough contents of each box. You could also keep your "master list" on your computer.

Auction Day!... Once a year, go through all the stuff you have stored and put aside items that you feel are of more value to someone else than to you. Place them on one of the Internet auction sites and buy something you really need with the proceeds.

Panty-Hose Protector... For a great way to store those left-over rolls of wallpaper and Christmas gift wrap, get out your old panty hose. Slip the rolls into the legs, peg the panty hose by the waist onto wire coat hangers and hang them up in a basement closet. No more frayed edges and a convenient way to store them!

See-Through Storage... If you can afford it, clear plastic containers are not only strong, but they're great for seeing exactly what you have stored.

Shrink Storage... Save all kinds of space when storing bulky items like blankets or pillows, etc. Take a plastic garbage bag and stuff it as full as you can get it with the items. Then hold the open end of the bag tightly around the nozzle of your vacuum cleaner and turn it on. As the air is sucked out, the filled bag will be reduced to about a quarter of its size. Spin the bag to prevent the air escaping, remove the nozzle and fold the now-twisted top of the bag over. Secure with a strong rubber band.

Step Storage... It shouldn't be too expensive to hire a carpenter to attach hinges to the top of each wood step leading down to your basement. The space inside the steps is great for storing items like out of season shoes, boots, winter wear, seasonal decorations, etc.

Travel Storage... For some reason, most people tend to store their empty suitcases...empty! Don't waste this valuable storage space. Keep your seasonal clothing folded neatly and carefully packed in the suitcases. If you need to use one or two for a vacation, simply store the clothing in a garbage bag until you return.

Screen Storage... An attractive folding screen, or two doors hinged together, in the corner of your basement can hold a multitude of storage sins behind it.

THE REST OF THE ROOMS

THE BATHROOM, LAUNDRY ROOM AND REC. ROOM...

The Bathroom... Get rid of all those bottles and containers that you use so rarely. You don't need 3 different types of shampoo and 4 different types of conditioner. Remember the more storage space you provide, the more you're likely to clutter it up!

♦ Once a month, make it a habit to check the expiration dates on the items in your medicine cabinet and replace those that have expired. If there isn't a date on them, call your pharmacist and ask his advice.

♦ If the sink in your bathroom is a pedestal sink, you can ensure you're never caught without toilet paper. 2 or 3 spare rolls tuck nicely into the back of most pedestals.

♦ Cut down on odor from your bathroom wastebasket by leaving a paper towel soaked in fabric softener in it.

The Laundry Room... Avoid huge piles of clothes after bringing them in from the clothesline. Hang them on the line in sections devoted to each family member. Fold the clothes in order and in separate piles and you'll be able to tuck them away neatly in their respective places immediately.

♦ A neat space-saving idea for your laundry room is to attach a wooden ironing board to the inside of the door. Depending on the height of your door, you may have to shorten the board slightly. Then simply remove the leg from the square end and screw that end to the door at a comfortable height with a large hinge. Trim the other leg to match the height of the hinged end and you have a convenient, foldaway ironing board.

The Recreation Room... While recreation rooms should feel lived in, that doesn't translate to being untidy. A clever way to avoid spending a lot of time keeping everything in its place is to use throw rugs and big scatter cushions. Strategically placed, they can hide all sorts of temporary clutter.

♦ Another idea to help cut down on clutter is to use furniture accents that can double for storage...wooden trunks as coffee tables, baskets for toys, books, blankets, etc. A cupboard or bookshelf with doors can simply be closed and the room will look tidier already.

♦ When designing your rec. room, consider running the wall paneling sideways, rather than up and down. It gives the impression of a much larger room.

~ ♦ ~

CHAPTER 10

INSIDE INFO ON THE OUTSIDE

CLEANING UP THE GREAT OUTDOORS!

GARDEN CLEANUP

WEEDS, WALLS AND WHATEVER...

Poisoning Poison Ivy... To clean out your garden of poison ivy, mix a solution of 3 parts salt, ¼ part dish soap and 2 parts hot water. Soak the ivy with the mixture 2 or 3 times.

Weeding Out Weeds... It will make your weeding job a lot easier if you wait until after a heavy or consistent rainfall before weeding.

♦ Remember, if you keep your lawn mowed regularly, it'll help prevent those lawn weeds from spreading their seeds.

♦ Commandeer your kid's plastic snow sled while he's not looking. It's great for carrying all the weeds you pull out. It's also really handy for carrying all those weeding tools, etc.

♦ A clever tool for weed removing is a beer-can opener. All you do is insert the opener under the root and lever it out.

Dandelion Dilemma... Have your dandelions already gone to seed? Get out in the garden with one of those gas BBQ lighters. Direct the flame onto the fluffy tops of the dandelions and burn the seeds before they can fly away and reproduce. Don't use this method on lawns where the grass is dry!

Bagging Leaves... Use your old bedsheets or a tarp to collect grass clipping or leaves by raking them onto the sheet. Then fold the sheet over the leaves and simply drag it away to your compost pile. Your back will thank you for it.

Compost Care... The most common cause of a composter giving off that offensive ammonia-type smell is usually too much wet or green material in it. So simply add some dry or brown material, like straw, dried grass or dried leaves, to it.

♦ If you add a large bottle of cola to your compost once a week or so, and turn it often, it should decompose the material faster. They say it also causes the compost to speed up seed germination and plant growth when used.

♦ Make sure you throw out weeds with large wandering roots. These roots may not break down as well as small roots and could cause weed problems in your garden down the road.

♦ If you place a length of 2-inch PVC pipe into your compost pile, it will ventilate it. It also makes it easier to add water to it if necessary.

Garden Walls... To get rid of marks and discoloration from brick walls, wet the wall thoroughly and rub a brick of the same color on the area.

♦ If you're having difficulty washing off the buildup and dust residue marks on your siding under the windows, try a little baking soda on a damp cloth. It often does the trick.

Planter Pointers... Whenever you're using old planters or pots be sure to clean them out really well before reusing. Do this with a solution of equal parts bleach and warm water. This will kill any mold or bacteria that could harm the plant.

Serious Seed Storage... Keep your toolshed free from scattered seed packet. Get one of those multidrawered nuts-and-bolts containers and store your seeds in the drawers. Simply label them accordingly.

Making The Moss Of It...
Sometimes it's necessary to realize that if you can't lick 'em, join 'em! If you find it's a continual battle to clean off areas of moss on your pottery planters, try this trick. Simply coat the outside surface with natural yogurt. In no time the entire planter will be covered in a luxuriant growth.

♦ If you have a moss problem on your lawn, however, remember that moss hates sweet soil. So sprinkle some lime on your lawn and keep that marauding moss off of it!

Cleaning Eaves Troughs... An old fan belt is an excellent tool for cleaning out your eaves trough. Because it's so flexible, it can take the exact shape of the eaves trough, and because it's tough, it can lift out whatever is in the eaves trough.

♦ You can prevent a lot of the leaves from jamming your down pipe by securing a plastic dish scourer over the hole.

Hose Hideaway... Store your garden hose in one of those half wooden barrels. It keeps it nice and organized. Accessible too!

♦ Or paint an old car tire with that granite-finish exterior paint so that it fits well with your garden décor. Feed your garden hose into the inside of the tire. It keeps it beautifully in place.

Cleaning Yourself... Scrub your hands and knees with a mixture of dish soap and a little sugar. Rinse off.

♦ Scrape your fingernails over a bar of hand soap before you start gardening. You'll find cleanup will be a lot easier.

UP AND DOWN THE GARDEN PATH

STEPPING-STONES, ETC....

Unwanted Growth?... A clever alternative to killing weeds between your patio stones is to replace the weeds with plants. Simply plant some attractive ground cover seeds between the walkway stones. They'll stunt the growth of any weeds as they proliferate.

♦ However, to simply discourage weed or grass growth in your stone patio or walkway, heat a gallon of water with a pound of salt. Stir well and pour between the stones.

♦ You can also pour undiluted white vinegar between
the stones.

♦ Or you can often inhibit the growth of weeds by pouring
a little borax and hot water between the stones at the
beginning of the season.

Unwanted Fall?... Your paving stones will last longer and
will be easier to clean in the spring if you don't use salt
to keep winter-ice off. Use fertilizer instead. It works
pretty well.

Walkway Art... If your
walkway slabs and
stones are really
looking shabby, give
them a new lease on
life by painting them.
Clean them thoroughly
first and then give
them a couple of coats
of good concrete
paint. If you want to
get a little more
creative, paint some
designs on them with
a stencil.

Concrete Cure... To remove those leaf stains from your
concrete patio or walkway, mix a solution of 1 quart water
and 1 cup bleach. Then thicken the mixture to a paste
by adding flour and smear it on the stained area. Let dry
and hose off.

♦ For greasy marks, mix a solution of 1 cup water softener and 1 gallon hot water and scrub well. If the stain persists, apply a paste of water and fuller's earth, let it sit on the stain for 24 hours and then hose it off.

♦ Or try scrubbing with a solution of 1 part water-less hand cleaner and 4 parts hot water. Hose it off afterward.

♦ Rust stains can often be removed by using some dry cement powder as a pumice and rubbing it with a piece of flagstone. The sandstone variety of flagstone is best.

Stone Stains... To spruce up your stone-covered areas, give the stone surface a good scrub with a solution of ¼ cup kerosene, 1 tablespoon regular dish soap and 1 gallon hot water.

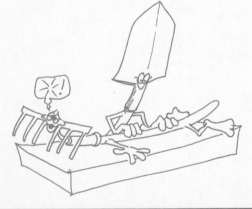

TOOL TREATMENTS

GARDEN-TOOL CARE AND STORAGE...

The Rust Of The Story... Store all your small garden tools, and the heads of your larger ones, in a mixture of fine sand and old motor oil. Some tools will fit in a bucket, but you may need a small tub for larger items.

♦ Sometimes light rust on tools can be removed by rubbing with a mixture of 2 parts salt and 1 part pure lemon juice. Heavier rust may require the use of fine steel wool as well.

Getting A Good Grip... You will find your wooden handles will last a lot longer if you clean them regularly with a cloth soaked in boiled linseed oil.

♦ A good way of protecting your tool handles is to slip on a piece of foam water-pipe insulation. Secure it with some duct tape.

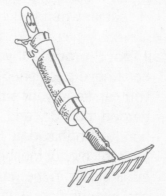

Sap Solution... Usually you can remove tree sap from the blades of your garden tools by simply rubbing them with a little rubbing alcohol.

Blade Care... For your bladed tools, like saws, clippers, etc., make sure you oil them regularly. Use either a good rust-inhibiting oil or, at the very least, a coating of petroleum jelly.

♦ Protect the easily damaged edge of your saw, shovel and hoe blades, with a homemade slip-on cover. All you need is a slit piece of good rubber hose placed over the edges!

♦ You can make your lawn-mower-blade cleaning job easier by spraying the blade with cooking-oil spray before each use. It helps prevent the grass clippings from adhering to it. And any that do, come off a lot easier when you clean them.

Mail Tool Storage... If you don't have a toolshed, you can keep your small garden tools dry and handy with this idea. Set a large colorful mailbox strategically in the garden and line the floor with dry sand and a little motor oil. Attractive and unique!

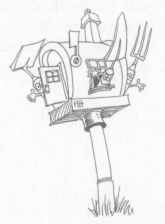

Toolbox Storage... Pick up an old carpenter's toolbox at a yard sale. It makes a great storage container for your small hand tools. It's also convenient for carrying them around your garden.

Ladder Safety Treatment... It's important to be able to detect any weak spots on your ladder, especially wooden ladders. Instead of hiding any potential trouble spots with paint, clean and maintain it with a good rubdown of boiled linseed oil every so often.

Panty Hose Potting... Cut down on that plastic-pot clutter in your toolshed with this great storage idea. Take a pair of old panty hose and cut a small hole out of the toe of each leg. Insert your plastic pots into the legs from the top and hang your panty-hose plant-pot protector from a wall or ceiling hook. Whenever you need a pot, simply slide it out the hole at the bottom of either leg.

PET CONTROL

FOUR-LEGGED FACTS...

Doggie Doo... Save yourself a messy cleanup job by discouraging dogs from using your garden as a toilet. Here's how to do it. Sprinkle a healthy amount of coarse black pepper in the garden bed. One sniff should do the trick!

Lawn Loiterers... To keep animals from leaving deposits on your lawn, spray problem areas with this potion. Mix 1 gallon water, 1 tablespoon cayenne pepper and ¼ cup Tabasco sauce.

Garbage Raiders... Keep animals like dogs and raccoons from tipping over your garbage and causing a messy cleanup with this method. Simply soak a rag in ammonia and tie it to the handles of the garbage can, as well as the lid.

Bath-Time Tip... The easiest way to bathe your pet is to put on a bathing suit and bathe him in the shower stall. At least you don't get your clothes wet!

♦ And if you don't have time to bathe him, you can occasionally give him a dry shampoo. All you do is rub some baking soda into the fur and brush his coat until the soda has been swept away along with the dirt. This is especially appreciated during those cold winter months.

Skunked Again!... If your dog has just had an encounter with a skunk, or rolled in something awful, and you've tried the usual methods of washing down with vinegar or tomato juice, to less of an effect than you would like, try this recipe. Mix 1 cup hydrogen peroxide, ½ teaspoon dish soap and 1 tablespoon baking soda. Apply to the dog's fur, taking care to cover his eyes. Let it dry on him. Throw away any leftover solution, as it is volatile and loses its effect after a while.

Removing Burrs... Using thick gloves, work either cooking oil or baby oil into the coat areas tangled with burrs. Breaking up the burrs with a pair of pliers, or something similar, also helps to remove them easier.

Removing Plaque... To clean your dog's teeth, simply tape a piece of gauze to the end of your forefinger. Wet the gauze and apply some baking soda to it. Brush away to your dog's content!

Dog-Dish Dilemma... To prevent your dog from upsetting his water bowl all the time, and you having to clean up the mess, use a Bundt pan to put his water in. Then drive a wooden or metal peg through the hole in the middle of the pan to hold it in place. Obviously this tip is for the outside only, unless, of course, you want holes in your floors!

OUTDOOR LIVING AND ENTERTAINING

BARBEQUES AND OUTDOOR FURNITURE...

BBQ Cleaning... A quick way to clean your BBQ grill is to place a sheet of aluminum foil on the grill, shiny side down. Turn the flame on high and leave the BBQ closed for a few minutes. Works on a similar principle to the self-cleaning oven.

♦ A good nonmessy way of cleaning your grill is to place it in a plastic garbage bag, throw in ¼ cup ammonia and tie it closed. Leave the bag laying flat outside overnight and hose it off the next day. It works great!

♦ Or you can just pop the grill in your self-cleaning oven and turn it on!

♦ Sometimes, if the grill is not too dirty, you can let it lay on the lawn overnight. If there's enough dew, it can loosen a lot of the burned-on food.

♦ Remember, if you spray your grill first with nonstick cooking oil, it'll make cleanup easier. Forethought is forearmed!

BBQ Spills... Here's a quick way to soak up those grease spills on your stone patio. Simply spread some kitty litter over the area and rub it in. Leave it on for a day or two, then rinse off.

Metal-Furniture Care... To add a protective layer to your metal outdoor furniture, simply apply a mixture of 5 parts petroleum jelly and 1 part lanolin.

♦ You can also apply a little mineral oil to the furniture, if you prefer.

♦ For winter storage, wipe with cooking oil and then wash off for the spring.

♦ To remove rust from badly rusted garden furniture, try this. Wrap the rusted part in a kerosene-soaked cloth for 2 or 3 days, then sand with medium sandpaper. Now you can paint the pieces as desired with a good rust paint.

Outdoor Resin Furniture... To remove grime from outdoor and patio plastic furniture, try this. Wearing rubber gloves, make up a solution of 8 parts bleach and 1 part dish soap. Wipe it on and let sit for 30 minutes. Rinse off well with clean water. Do NOT follow with a cleaner that has ammonia as an ingredient.

♦ You can also try rubbing the furniture with baking soda
on a damp cloth.

♦ Sometimes, for
stubborn stains
you need to make
a paste of baking
soda and water
and leave it on
until it dries.
Scour off well
with water.

Outdoor Wooden Furniture... Remove that mildew from
your wooden patio furniture by making a solution of 4
tablespoon of baking soda, ½ cup of white distilled vinegar
and 1 cup of ammonia. Pour this mixture into a bucket of
warm water and scrub down the furniture with it.

Patio Umbrella... You can literally double the life of your patio
umbrella by storing it properly through the winter. Stretch
one leg of a pair of panty hose over the umbrella and tie
the other leg around the handle to hold it in place. This
not only keeps it snug as a bug in a rug all winter long,
it also allows the umbrella to breath, which inhibits mold.
In addition, it also stops spiders from nesting in the folds.

Deck Mold... To remove mold from your wooden deck,
wash it down with full-strength apple-cider vinegar. Let sit
for 2 hours or so and then rinse with clean water, or it'll
attract flies.

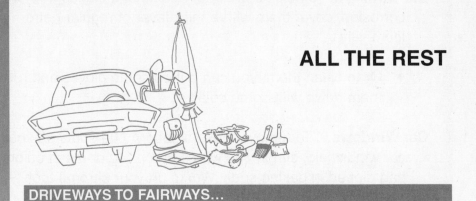

ALL THE REST

DRIVEWAYS TO FAIRWAYS...

Asphalt Driveways... Wash down with liquid dish detergent and water.

Concrete Driveways... Oil spills on concrete driveway surfaces can usually be soaked up by spreading powdered cement over the spill. Once the spill has been soaked up, apply a little dish soap and hose down.

Garage Floors... Remove oil drippings from concrete garage floors by first placing several layers of newspaper over the stain. Soak the paper with water and allow it to dry. If the stain persists, scrub with mineral oil or kerosene. Wash down immediately with detergent and water.

Exhaust Blues... To remove the blue overheating stains on your motorcycle exhaust, wash it down with vinegar while it is still hot. Be sure to wear gloves and eyewear to protect yourself.

Engine Cleaning... A great engine cleaner for cars and motorcycles is a mixture of 1 part waterless hand cleaner and 4 parts hot water. Pour the solution into a spray bottle and apply the spray to the engine. Hose off afterward.

Car Battery... To help keep battery posts and cables free of corrosion, cover them with a thick layer of regular petroleum jelly.

♦ Or to clean them, you can put on some gloves and rub them down with some cola!

Car Windows... To remove those stubborn bug spots on your car windshield, simply rub with a damp rag or mesh onion bag dipped in baking soda. Works on your chrome too!

Chrome Cleaner... Apply baking soda on a damp sponge or cloth. Leave for an hour or so and then rinse off with water and dry.

♦ Or dampen a soft cloth with ammonia and wipe your chrome down. Rinse with clean water and buff to a shine.

♦ To remove minor rust marks from your chrome bumpers, simply rub them with aluminum foil wet with cola.

Upholstery Cleaner... For car upholstery and carpets, see "Carpet And Rug Shampoo."

Instant Wipes... Keep a package of baby wet wipes in your glove compartment. They are great for cleaning up all kinds of accidental messes.

Air Freshener... Tuck a few fabric-softener sheets under the seats to reduce car odor.

Paint Spatters… You can remove small dried paint spatters from windows by simply scraping them off with an ordinary penny. Be gentle though!

Paint Roller Trays… Before you pour the paint into your roller tray, slip a plastic shopping bag over the tray. This acts as a liner, which can be removed mess free when inverted as it is pulled off. Behold…a perfectly pristine paint tray!

Paintbrushes… Restore hardened paintbrushes by soaking them for 2 or 3 days in a solution of ½ cup kerosene, ¼ cup salt and 4 cups water. Brush the bristles with a fork or comb.

 ♦ Pure hot vinegar often softens bristles too. Leave the brush in overnight.

Paint Handles… When painting ceilings, prevent the paint from running down the handle and onto your hands by slip- ping a sponge over the handle first. Any dripping paint will be caught in the sponge.

Paint Hands… If you rub your hands with petroleum jelly before painting, you should be able to wash the paint off easily with soap and water afterward. This also makes cleanup easier from window glass when painting the panes.

Awnings... Canvas awnings should be scrubbed down with a hard-bristled brush and some laundry soap. Hose down well.

Gleaming Golf Balls... Mix a solution of 1 gallon water and 1 cup ammonia. Leave your golf balls in the solution overnight.

Golf Clubs... Get a grip on your game by having clean club grips. Scrub them with toothpaste and wash them with a little soap and water. Dry well.

♦ Club shafts sometimes need a buff with a little paint thinner to make them shine.

~ ♦ ~

CHAPTER 11

YOU AND YOURS FROM
TOP TO BOTTOM

CLEANING AND ORGANIZING...YOURSELF AND
YOUR POSSESSIONS!

GETTING PERSONAL

HAIR HINTS...

Shampoo Buildup... Constant shampooing can leave a soap buildup on your scalp. Every so often, rinsing with a cup of apple-cider vinegar will help to cleanse your scalp.

Dry Shampoo... If you don't have time to wash your hair, just mix 1 part salt and 8 parts cornmeal. Apply it to your hair and brush it out.

Shampoo Substitute... If you run out of hair shampoo, you can always use 1 part mild dishwashing liquid and 4 parts water until you get to the store.

Clever Conditioner... Here's a wonderful conditioner for virtually all types of hair. Simply massage in some peppermint oil.

♦ Another all-round conditioner and deep cleanser is eucalyptus oil.

Gummy Hair... To remove sticky chewing gum from your hair, put the white of an egg on it and work the gum out with your fingers.

Hair-Dye Prevention... To prevent dye from staining your skin, rub a little petroleum jelly on your skin around the hairline.

Hair-Dye Cure... Sometimes rubbing fresh hair dye on areas where you have dried hair dye will remove the stain on your skin.

♦ Believe it or not, you can also try rubbing your skin with cigarette ash.

Pool Pointer... To keep your hair from being damaged by the combination of pool chemicals and sun, apply equal parts suntan lotion and hair conditioner to your hair. Wash out after swimming.

♦ To remove the green tinge that pool chemicals can give your hair, apply a mixture of 1 part lemon juice and 6 parts water.

BODY HINTS...

Keep It Kosher... For a good body exfoliant, use kosher salt and water.

Milk Bath... Take a leaf out of Cleopatra's book. Add a full cup of powdered milk to your hot bathwater, lie back and soak it in. This little treat should make your skin feel silky smooth afterward.

Aftershave... For a great homemade aftershave lotion for your legs, try mixing this recipe: 1 cup water, ¼ cup rubbing alcohol, ¼ cup glycerin, ¼ cup witch hazel, ½ teaspoon alum, ¼ teaspoon baking soda, 2 or 3 drops of your favorite perfume.

♦ Always rinse your legs in cold water immediately after shaving your legs.

Out Of Shave... Run out of shaving cream? Baby oil works in a pinch!

Easy Back Washer... For an effective way to wash your back in the shower or bathtub, take a leg of panty hose and position a bar of bath soap halfway inside the leg. Secure the bar of soap from moving with a single knot on either side of the soap. Use your "hose washer" to wash your back, the same way as you would normally towel your back dry.

Foot Fact... Eucalyptus oil rubbed into your feet can prevent foot odor for quite some time.

Tool Tip... You should always keep your cleaning tools, like sponges, facecloths and loofahs, clean. Rinse them out well and hang to dry. Give them a restoration treatment once a month or so as well. Soak them in equal parts white vinegar and water overnight. Wash them out well and hang them up to dry.

FACE HINTS...

Cleansers... Want a wonderful face cleanser? Mix up a paste of oatmeal, yogurt and water. Apply the mixture to your face, let sit for 10 minutes, then rinse off with cool water.

♦ Or make a thick paste of baking soda and water. Massage it into your skin for a minute or two, then rinse off with cool water.

Facial Rinse... You'll love this fragrant recipe for a facial rinse, to remove soap film after washing your face. Mix together 1 tablespoon dried rosemary, 2 tablespoons rose petals, 2 tablespoons chamomile flowers and 1 quart of water. Boil the mixture in a glass or enamel pot (uncovered) for about 10 minutes or so. Let cool, strain the solid ingredients out and decant the liquid into a spray mister. Keep well refrigerated.

Moisturizer... Want an effective and inexpensive face moisturizer? Simply throw a banana and some milk into your blender and blend it smooth. Apply the mixture to your face and leave it on for half an hour or so. Rinse off with cool water.

♦ Another excellent moisturizer is a combination of 2 tablespoons of olive oil, 2 tablespoons of coconut oil, 2 tablespoons regular vegetable cooking oil and ¼ cup of mashed ripe strawberries. Cover and store in the fridge. Good for about 1 week.

Makeup Removal... Try to avoid using tissues to clean off your eye makeup. Some of them have wood products in their composition that can irritate your eyes. Use cotton balls or pads instead.

Spot Removal... For small pimples, clean them out by pressing a cotton ball dipped in hot water and a little salt for about 2 minutes.

Eye Opener... Many experts agree that it's not a good idea to use soap to clean around the eye area. It'll tend to dry it out.

Breath Freshener... Here's a great freshening mouthwash. Just mix 1 teaspoon salt and 1 teaspoon baking soda in a glass of warm water.

What...No Toothpaste?... Mix together some baking soda, table salt and a little extract of peppermint and brush away!

WARDROBE WISDOM

CLEVER CLOTHING CARE...

Fresh Fragrance... Wrap a small amount of lavender in a piece of muslin. Tie it with a ribbon and hang it up in your clothes closet.

- ◆ Or tie 2 or 3 fabric softener sheets onto a coat hanger and hang it up.

Fresh Drawer Fragrance... Here's a great idea to make your own scented drawer liners. Haul out that leftover wallpaper (you can even match the paper in your bedroom) and spray it with a little of your favorite perfume. Let it dry completely and line your drawer with it.

- ◆ If you prefer you can use an essential oil like lavender, apple, strawberry, etc. Have some fun experimenting with different scents.

- ◆ Little lavender bundles wrapped in cheesecloth will give off a great fragrance in your lingerie drawer.

Dry Uncleaning... It's a good idea not to keep your clothes in those plastic dry-cleaner bags for too long. They can develop a yellowish color.

Cedar Stain... If you use cedar chips in your closet, try to keep the clothes from coming into direct contact with them for any length of time. Cedar chips can sometimes cause a discoloration on clothing.

Hanger Stain... Try to use padded, wood or plastic coat hangers. Hangers made of wire can cause marks on the clothes.

Hanger Crease... Take the card-board core from the center of an aluminum-foil or paper-towel roll and slit it down its length. Slip it over your wire coat hanger's base to prevent your pants and trousers developing a sharp crease across the legs.

Tie Trick... Next time, when you bring a new tie home, spray it with a little upholstery guard. It'll make removing spills a lot easier.

♦ To spiff up your silk ties, simply hang them in the bathroom while you're having a hot shower; the steam should do the trick!

♦ To clean your silk ties, wait until you have boiled potatoes for dinner. Let the water cool to luke warm, dip a sponge into it and carefully dab the tie clean.

Hat Trick... No place to hang your good hat? Use an ordinary coffee can. It's just the right size to place your hat over. You can decorate it to suit your style.

Smelly Shoe Trick... Simply leave a used fabric-softener sheet inside each shoe.

White-Shoe Shine... Give the shoe a wipe with a soft cloth and a little ammonia. Works on white canvas shoes as well.

♦ Another canvas-shoe brightener is talcum powder. Sprinkle a little on a brush and rub the shoe with it.

♦ A little white toothpaste rubbed on your white shoes will remove most scuff marks quickly and easily. Buff with old panty hose after for a great shine!

Patent-Shoe Shine... For a mirror finish on patent-leather shoes, apply some baby oil or furniture polish. Buff with a paper towel or soft cloth.

♦ Most scuff marks can be removed from patent leather with an ordinary eraser.

Quick Shoe Shine... In a pinch, just rub your shoes with a little hand cream. Buff afterward.

Suede... Removing a stubborn stain on suede can be quite simple. If ordinary brushing doesn't do the trick, try rubbing the spot lightly with an emery board, then steam over a boiling kettle. Just like new. Be careful with that steam though!

♦ Sometimes on light suede colors a little rubbing alcohol on a cloth might do the trick. Always test for colorfastness first though.

♦ Many makeup stains can be removed from suede jacket collars by rubbing the stain with a heel of bread.

Treating Your Old Bag... To keep the metal shining on your purse, why not give the metal a protective nail polish coating.

Leather Salt Stains... To remove those leather salt stains you get on your boots and shoes in the winter, simply cut a onion in half and rub away the stain.

THE DRESSING TABLE

TRINKETS AND TREASURES...

Brushes And Comb Cleaning... A quick and easy way is to pop them into the sink and then fill it up with hot water. Add about 2 tablespoons ammonia and 2 teaspoons dish soap. Let them sit for 15 minutes, rinse them off and let them air-dry.

♦ Another method is to add equal parts baking soda and bleach to a sink of warm water. Rinse well and let them air-dry.

Eyeglass Cleaning...
Believe it or not, a little vodka on a soft cloth is a great way to clean the untreated lenses of your eyeglasses. One tot should do it!

Amber... Put a small amount of mineral oil on a soft cloth and rub your amber gently. Buff with a soft dry cloth.

Pearls Of Wisdom... Clean your pearl jewelry with a little olive oil on a soft cloth.

Opals... Take care when cleaning your opals. Be sure to never use soap or detergent . Simply give them a soft brush with warm water only.

Lapis And Turquoise... Both beautiful stones that can be cleaned easily. Use a soft clean cloth dipped in a little cool water and detergent. Rub gently. Never use soap.

Cameo Appearance... Mix a solution of ¼ teaspoon dish soap, 3 drops ammonia and ½ cup warm water. Dampen a soft cloth with the mixture and dab it carefully on your cameo. Dry the piece off with a dry lintless cloth or, preferably, a chamois.

Silver Jewelry... Rub with a soft cloth dipped in baking soda. A toothbrush may be needed for those small areas. Once cleaned, rinse well and buff dry.

Gold Jewelry... Make a homemade solution of 2 tablespoons liquid hand soap, one cup warm water and ½ teaspoon ammonia. Wipe the solution onto the gold piece with a lint-free cloth. Buff dry.

♦ Another quick cleaner for your gold jewelry is rubbing alcohol. Rub it on with a soft cloth.

Diamond Jewelry... Mix 2 cups of water, 4 drops ammonia and 1 tablespoon soap flakes and bring them to a boil. Place the item in a tea strainer and hold it in the solution for 3 seconds only. Remove it and rinse it off in cool water.

Glass Beads... Rinse them in a solution of equal parts vinegar and water.

Costume Jewelry... Pop them into a container of warm water and throw in a denture tablet. Rinse off well and dry.

~ ♦ ~

CHAPTER 12

EASY-FIND INDEX

THE MOST IMPORTANT PART OF
THE BOOK! FIND THE EXACT
HINT YOU WANT INSTANTLY!

H

Y

COMMON CONVERSIONS

VOLUME

Approximations:

5 milliliters	=	⅙ ounce	=	1 teaspoon
15 milliliters	=	½ ounce	=	1 tablespoon
50 milliliters	=	1½ ounces	=	¼ cup
100 milliliters	=	3 ounces	=	½ cup
175 milliliters	=	5¼ ounces	=	¾ cup
250 milliliters	=	7½ ounces	=	1 cup

3 teaspoons	=	1 tablespoon
4 tablespoons	=	¼ cup
8 tablespoons	=	½ cup
1 cup	=	½ pint
1 cup	=	8 ounces
4 cups	=	1 quart

Knowing	Multiply By	To Obtain
teaspoons	5	milliliters
tablespoons	15	milliliters
fluid ounces	30	milliliters
cups	0.24	liters
pints	0.56	liters
quarts	1.1	liters
gallons	4.5	liters
milliliters	0.03	fluid ounces
liters	1.75	pints
liters	0.87	quarts
liters	0.22	gallons

GLOSSARY OF TERMS

NORTH AMERICAN	–	EUROPEAN
broiler	–	grill
club soda	–	soda water
cornstarch	–	corn flour
denatured alcohol	–	methylated spirits
drapery	–	curtains
eaves trough	–	guttering
faucet	–	tap
garbage bags	–	refuse sacks
garbage disposer	–	waste disposal
gum/Artgum eraser	–	rubber
kerosene	–	paraffin
lard	–	shortening
latex paint	–	emulsion
liquid dish soap	–	washing-up liquid
pants	–	trousers
plastic baggies	–	small plastic bags
purse	–	handbag
registers	–	vents
rubbing alcohol	–	isopropyl alcohol
screening	–	wire mesh
shower stall	–	shower cubicle
toque	–	knitted hat
washing soda*	–	water softener, lime-scale remover
waxed paper	–	greaseproof

*IMPORTANT: The silver-cleaning hint on page 38 refers to "washing soda." Do not use washing soda crystals. They can react with the aluminum foil causing noxious fumes. Use powdered lime-scale remover (sometimes called water softener) sold for use in washing machines.

ACKNOWLEDGMENTS

Our grateful thanks to the following people who contributed so much of their time, expertise and knowledge to the content of this book.

CARMAN ARICO

MARY ELIN ARICO

JAAN ARTHURS

BARB BALLANTYNE

NANCY BIRCH

GAIL BOND

LARRY BOND

STEVE BROWN

CATHERINE CLARK

ALEX DAHR

STEVEN EPSTEIN

CATHY HANSEN

LENI HENDERSON

MITCHELL HEWSON

PATRICIA JOHNSON

DARLENE JONES

DONNA JONES

LAURAL JONES

MICHELLE KARKER

HEIDY LAWRANCE

RUTH MADDOCK

MENARY FAMILY

ANDY MOREAU

LYNNE MOREAU

PHAEDRA POVEY

JOEL SANFIL

JOHN SUDNIKOWICZ

LETITIA TANNER

ALISON TRANBARGER EPSTEIN

ADAM WHITE

HAROLD WHITE

Your Personal Hint Collection